Cambridge Elements ☰

Elements in Ancient and Pre-modern Economies
edited by
Kenneth G. Hirth
The Pennsylvania State University
Timothy Earle
Northwestern University
Emily J. Kate
University of Vienna

ECONOMIES OF THE INCA WORLD

R. Alan Covey
The University of Texas at Austin
Jordan A. Dalton
SUNY Oswego

CAMBRIDGE
UNIVERSITY PRESS

Shaftesbury Road, Cambridge CB2 8EA, United Kingdom

One Liberty Plaza, 20th Floor, New York, NY 10006, USA

477 Williamstown Road, Port Melbourne, VIC 3207, Australia

314–321, 3rd Floor, Plot 3, Splendor Forum, Jasola District Centre,
New Delhi – 110025, India

103 Penang Road, #05–06/07, Visioncrest Commercial, Singapore 238467

Cambridge University Press is part of Cambridge University Press & Assessment,
a department of the University of Cambridge.

We share the University's mission to contribute to society through the pursuit of
education, learning and research at the highest international levels of excellence.

www.cambridge.org
Information on this title: www.cambridge.org/9781009552134

DOI: 10.1017/9781009552080

When citing this work, please include a reference to the DOI 10.1017/9781009552080

First published 2025

A catalogue record for this publication is available from the British Library

ISBN 978-1-009-55213-4 Hardback
ISBN 978-1-009-55209-7 Paperback
ISSN 2754-2955 (online)
ISSN 2754-2947 (print)

Economies of the Inca World

Elements in Ancient and Pre-modern Economies

DOI: 10.1017/9781009552080
First published online: January 2025

R. Alan Covey
The University of Texas at Austin

Jordan A. Dalton
SUNY Oswego

Author for correspondence: R. Alan Covey, r.alan.covey@austin.utexas.edu

Abstract: The Inca Empire (c. 1400–1532) was the largest Indigenous state to develop in the Americas, spanning the extraordinarily rich landscapes of the central Andes. Scholarly approaches to Inca-era economies initially drew on Spanish colonial documents that emphasized royal resource monopolies, labor tribute, and kin-based land tenure. Anthropologists in recent decades have emphasized local economic self-sufficiency and the role of reciprocity in Inca economics. This Element adds to the existing literature by reviewing recent archaeological research in the Inca capital region and different provinces. The material evidence and documents indicate considerable variation in the development and implementation of Inca political economy, reflecting an array of local economic practices that were tailored to different Andean environments. Although Inca economic development downplayed interregional trade, emerging evidence indicates the existence of more specialized trading practices in Inca peripheral regions, some of which persisted under imperial rule.

Keywords: Inca Empire, political economy, reciprocity, modes of exchange, subsistence practices

ISBNs: 9781009552134 (HB), 9781009552097 (PB), 9781009552080 (OC)
ISSNs: 2754-2955 (online), 2754-2947 (print)

Contents

1 The Inca Empire and Andean Economics

Around 1615, an Andean nobleman named Felipe Guaman Poma de Ayala illustrated the first economic encounter between Inca and Spaniard – an imagined event that would have occurred some eighty years earlier, when Francisco Pizarro and his band of *conquistadores* invaded the Andes and carried off a king's ransom in gold and silver (Figure 1). The drawing shows the Inca Huayna Capac meeting the Greek artilleryman Pedro de Candía in the royal palace in Cuzco, the imperial capital. Seated on a low throne, the Inca hands the kneeling Candía a shallow plate of gold nuggets and gestures at lavish serving vessels placed between them, asking in Quechua: "Do you eat this gold?" (*Cay coritachu mihunqui?*). Grasping the treasure, the *conquistador* affirms in Spanish: "We eat this gold" (*Este oro comemos*).

Historians agree that this encounter never actually occurred, but it vividly illustrates the economic uncertainties accompanying the European invasion and colonization, and the ongoing challenge of translating Andean concepts of value and exchange into European ones. In this *Element*, we place the Inca political economy into its rich prehistoric and geographical context, identifying how the empire sought to bind together a large portion of South America's Andean region from around 1400 until the European invasions of the 1530s. Andean ecological and cultural diversity inspire an emphasis on "economies of the Inca world," an array of local subsistence and exchange practices that did not all fit neatly under the administrative goals of the conquering empire. Inca strategies to integrate ten million or more subjects living across diverse and challenging landscapes offer important points of comparison with the economic policies of other early empires. Andean economies also present significant contrasts with the mercantilist and capitalist practices that accompanied Spanish colonization.

To approach Inca-era economies using Andean cultural values, Section 1 offers an introduction to early colonial Quechua terminology and concepts used throughout this Element. Section 2 then addresses the retrospective accounts of the Inca world authored by (mostly) Spanish writers and more recent scholarly studies of Andean life. Colonial descriptions of Inca political economy vary, and historians and anthropologists have recast them in light of modern economic values, often treating the absence of familiar practices – coinage, labor markets, real estate – as evidence of underdevelopment or insurmountable cultural difference. Archaeological research offers a growing database for reconsidering Inca political economy and local Andean practices of reciprocity and redistribution. Evidence collected from multiple Andean regions reorients attention to the dynamic negotiations occurring as the Incas incorporated diverse local societies and landscapes into the largest empire to form in the ancient Americas (Figure 2).

Figure 1 Felipe Guaman Poma de Ayala's imagined encounter between Inca and *conquistador. El primer nueva corónica [y buen gobierno conpuesto por Don Phelipe Guaman Poma de Ayala, señor y príncipe]* (c. 1615), GKS 2232 folio, Royal Danish Library, p. 369[371]/drawing 147.

The remaining four sections of this *Element* present case studies that trace the developmental arc of Inca political economy in different social and ecological settings. Section 3 describes early Inca growth and the consolidation of a "noble

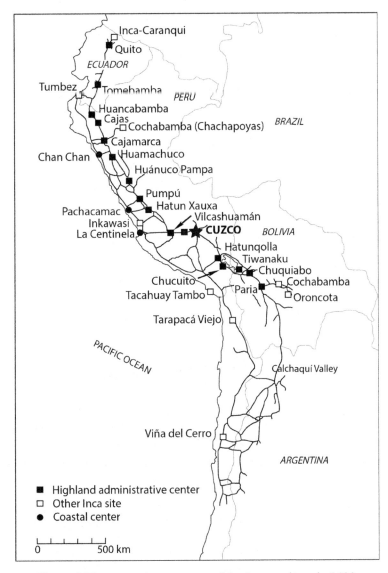

Figure 2 The approximate extent of the Inca territory in 1530.

economy" in the region surrounding Cuzco, whereas Section 4 reviews the imperial economies of the nearby highland provinces. The last two sections range farther from the imperial center, exploring economic networks of the Pacific coast (Section 5) and the organization of frontier and peripheral regions (Section 6). Each of these sections combines the available written and material evidence to reconstruct local and imperial interactions. Colonial documents describe Inca conquests and the development of infrastructure and tribute practices in many provincial regions. Archaeological excavations, surveys, and laboratory analyses contribute material evidence of the Inca political economy, including contexts that Spanish writers could not accurately describe, such as pre-Inca subsistence and exchange practices and the changing dynamics of household economies under Inca rule.

The Incas expanded from the highlands of Cuzco, in what is today southern Peru, rapidly building a vast empire that they called Tawantinsuyu, which in Quechua means "the whole comprising four parts together" (for a recent overview, see D'Altroy 2014). Those four parts included Chinchaysuyu to the northwest, Antisuyu to the east, Collasuyu to the southeast, and Contisuyu to the southwest. The Inca people of Cuzco claimed the authority to civilize diverse Andean landscapes and their inhabitants. Inca rulers used their subjects' labor to transform local lands – building roads, storehouses, and new valley-bottom fields – and they reorganized subject populations for easier administration. While establishing new administrative officials, the Incas instituted or reinforced social structures that were familiar to them, such as the division of communities and ethnic groups into complementary upper (*hanan*) and lower (*hurin*) halves.

The imperial expansion chronology is currently undergoing reassessment to account for new radiocarbon dates indicating an Inca presence in some distant provinces (e.g., northwest Argentina) by around 1400 (Figure 3). The new dates challenge a long-accepted model drawn from colonial chronicles that identifies the ninth *Sapa Inca*, Pachacuti Inca Yupanqui, as the first to lead campaigns beyond the Cuzco region, around 1438. Those sources describe how Pachacuti's son (Topa Inca Yupanqui) and grandson (Huayna Capac) enlarged the empire and consolidated provincial rule across the Andes. After Huayna Capac's

	INCAS	COYAS
AD 1000		
Mythical origins	Manco Capac	Mama Huaco
	Sinchi Roca	Mama Coca
Local alliances	Lloque Yupanqui	Mama Caua
	Mayta Capac	Mama Taucaray
	Capac Yupanqui	Mama Chuqui Illpay
Expansion beyond Cuzco region	Inca Roca	Mama Micay
	Yahuar Huaccac	Mama Chiquia
	Viracocha Inca	Mama Runtucayan
	Pachacuti Inca Yupanqui	Mama Anahuarque
Provincial Consolidation	Tupa Inca Yupanqui	Mama Ocllo
	Huayna Capac	Raua Ocllo
Civil War	Huascar/Atahualpa	Chuqui Huipa
AD 1532		

Figure 3 The Inca dynasty, according to 1540s testimony of *quipu* specialists.

unexpected death, a succession crisis erupted into a civil war between his sons Huascar and Atahualpa. Pizarro's expedition entered the Andean highlands in 1532, just as Atahualpa's forces prevailed in this destructive conflict. The *conquistadores* captured Atahualpa at the imperial center of Cajamarca, held him hostage while they extorted a ransom of gold and silver, and then killed him before marching southward to occupy Cuzco.

Before the Inca civil war, the empire dominated the Andean region between what is today southern Colombia and central Chile. The intensity of imperial governance varied across the realm, but some common hallmarks of the Inca political economy were broadly instituted. Some writers stated that the empire reorganized farmland and camelid herds after conquering new highland provinces, designating resources for the Inca and the sun cult alongside those of local communities and their lords (*curacas*). After establishing the new system of land tenure, the imperial state mobilized the labor of subject populations for the construction of new infrastructure, as well as farming, herding, and mining for the ruler and the state religion. Most productive work was done locally, but the empire also resettled workers (*mitimaes*) to perform specific tasks in nearby towns or far-flung provinces, providing necessary tools and subsistence for nonlocal projects (Hu and Quave 2020). The name of these resettled workers comes from *mit'a*, a traditional Andean form of rotational labor. In principle, groups of colonist households provided extended rounds of work to the Inca on behalf of the kin groups and villages with whom they shared tributary obligations. In practice, many of these "rotational" workers moved permanently from their provincial homes, settling at planned towns in the Cuzco region, frontier garrisons, and Inca-established artisan communities in provincial areas (see Section 5). The power to relocate substantial populations is a hallmark of other early empires (e.g., Assyrian, Roman) and a practice that continued in more recent ones, which established imperial outposts in locations as remote as Siberia and Australia.

While modifying traditional labor practices for state purposes, the Incas also created special statuses, including *mama*, *yana*, and *camayo(c)*. The *mamacona* were priestesses who trained selected young women (called *acllacona*) to produce Inca-style textiles, food, and maize beer, which they dispensed at state festivities and offered as sacrifices in temples and shrines. For the everyday labor that supported palaces and temples, the Incas designated thousands of households as *yanacona*, unfree workers whom the Spaniards called "perpetual servants" because they were not bought and sold like the chattel slaves of that time. Inca rulers took *yanacona* from groups that either fought or rebelled against them, settling most in the capital region, where early colonial administrators documented substantial *yana* populations (Covey and Amado 2008). The Cuzco region was also home to specialized laborers who embodied skilled tasks that we think of as "craft specialization." Called *camayos* in the chronicles, these artisans were experts in dye-making, potting, weaving, and metalworking, as well as other sustained labors, such as salt production and special farming and herding tasks. The Incas established communities of *camayos* in some provinces, where their specific occupations fulfilled tributary obligations to the state.

As they developed their tributary mode of production, Inca rulers also established a hierarchy of officials to enact sovereign demands on remote rural landscapes. Chronicle accounts of Inca administration describe tributary households in some highland regions as being organized into decimal hierarchies that ranged from units as small as 5 households to provinces of 10,000. Decimal administration was rooted in finger-counting, and the term for an official, *curaca*, is also glossed as "thumb" and "eldest son" in the earliest Quechua dictionary. Pairing the households counted out on each hand created a unit of 10 (*chunca*), which could then be counted out 5 times to create another unit (*pisca chunca*, or 50) that was paired to make the *pachaca*, or 100 households. A complement of 10 *pachaca* (2 groups of 500) constituted a *huaranca*, and 10 *huaranca* represented the ideal province size, called an *hunu*.

Colonial writers indicate different kinds of power, authority, and obligation across the decimal hierarchy (Cobo 1892:233 [1653 bk. 12 ch. 25]). Governors (*apu*) who were close relatives of the Inca ruler administered most *hunu* units and larger provincial groupings (*suyu*), delivering tribute demands, conducting inspections, and punishing serious crimes on his behalf. Officials reporting to an *apu* came from the governed population and held *curaca* titles tied to the size of their administrative units (e.g., *huaranca curaca*, administrator of 1,000 households). *Curaca* officials were not full-time administrators, but they provided "middle management" and were charged with implementing Inca demands. By contrast, the local officials, called *camayo* (e.g., *chunca camayo*, responsible for ten households), would have worked to convince their relatives, neighbors, and subjects to comply with Inca demands, balancing them against the schedules and social expectations of local labor practices. Inca officials reviewed changes in tributary populations, herd sizes, and inventories of goods in imperial storehouses, sometimes using a device called a *yupana* to make calculations. They encoded information using the *quipu*, a knotted-cord device maintained by provincial record-keepers (*quipucamayos*). The empire used message-runners called *chasqui* to convey information between regions, maintaining posts at regular intervals along the thousands of kilometers of royal roads that connected Cuzco to major provincial centers.

Where it was implemented, decimal organization promoted a political economy that mobilized tributary labor to produce a variety of staple and wealth goods. Terence D'Altroy and Timothy Earle (1985:188) describe staple finance as "the obligatory payments in kind to the state of subsistence goods such as grain, livestock, and clothing," whereas wealth finance consists of "the manufacture and procurement of special products," including valuable goods and money. Inca wealth goods included decorated pottery, fine textiles, and metal tools and adornments (Figure 4). While stressing the importance of staple finance for generating state surpluses across Inca highland provinces, D'Altroy and Earle also note the tributary collection of wealth goods, which the empire used to build relationships with provincial elites, especially in marginal regions where staple finance was less well developed (see Earle 1994). Local groups engaged in the production and distribution of staple and wealth finance in different ways across the Andes, with variable impacts on their subsistence economies, exchange practices, and status displays.

Figure 4 Inca narrow-neck jar (*urpu*), Metropolitan Museum of Art (1978.412.68).

One way to approach how Andean peoples thought about their economic lives in Inca times is through the economic vocabulary recorded in the oldest surviving Quechua dictionary, published by the Dominican friar Domingo de Santo Tomás in 1560. Although lacking entries for commerce (*comercio*), money (*dinero*), and coinage (*moneda*), the lexicon lists terms for property and wealth (*yma ayca*), exchange value (*chani*), luxury (*chapi*), and debt (*piñasni*), suggesting that Andean conceptualizations of these principles existed in Inca times. Quechua economic vocabulary situates such concepts within social contexts. It distinguishes a rich person (*capac*) from a poor one (*guaccha*) in terms of social connections and power, rather than material prosperity. It differentiates between possession of a common resource (*chapayay*) and ownership, which is linked to hereditary lordship (*yayanc*). The lexicon identifies communal landholding, using the Spanish word *heredad* (inheritance) to gloss terms for agricultural plots (*chacara*, *chapa*) and boundary markers (*sayua*). Its entries for tribute use the verb *cacay*, associated with the term for maternal uncle, underscoring the role of kinship in mobilizing labor for elite projects. Beyond kin-based economic relations, the dictionary also describes a transactional economy based on barter (*randini*) that might take place in a temporary marketplace (*catu*). There are terms for a range of artisans (*camayoc*), whose workshops produced cloth, pottery, silver, and unguents; as well as vendors or merchants working in the marketplace (*catu camayoc*).

This lexicon is consistent with early colonial descriptions of Indigenous economic practices in Cuzco and the central Andean highlands, but it does not represent those found in other parts of the Andes, such as the Pacific coast and the Amazonian lowlands, which were ecologically and linguistically distinct. Long-distance trading was much more pronounced in many peripheral regions. For example, in Ecuador there existed merchants called *mindalaes* who moved goods between lowlands and highlands, using strands of colorful shell beads called *chaquira* as a medium of interregional exchange. We will return to the *mindalaes* – as well as traders who sailed the Pacific coast or sponsored llama caravans that traversed the south-central Andes – in Sections 5 and 6.

2 Inca Political Economy in Historical Context

As archaeologists and ethnohistorians collect new evidence about Inca-era economies, their work builds on, and is influenced by, a long history of colonial discourse and academic analysis. There are no pre-contact records describing Inca economic organization, so the earliest written descriptions come from Spanish eyewitnesses and early colonial officials, who authored new accounts well into the 1600s. Colonial interpretations set the agenda for scholarly studies published after Spain's American colonies gained independence in the early 1800s. Economists and political scientists used colonial accounts of Inca economic control to portray the empire as less advanced than Western states, whereas anthropological scholarship produced since the 1940s addresses Inca economics in terms of distinctive practices that were highly tailored to highland Andean cultures and landscapes.

Early Descriptions

Charles V, the Holy Roman Emperor who ruled Spain from 1516 to 1556, sent Francisco Pizarro to Peru as a colonist in 1529, imagining that he and 250 other Spaniards would establish a kingdom called New Castile within the lands of Andean lords, using Indigenous labor to deliver steady revenues to the Crown from taxes, tribute, and mining output. These goals reflected late medieval economic practices in Europe, where the Church and nobility dominated rural land tenure and attempted to regulate the increasing commerce of growing cities and trade networks. Instead of settling as colonists, Pizarro and his men rampaged through the Andes, carrying off whatever wealth they could extort. The *conquistadores* did not actually eat gold, but their appetite for the metal was voracious (Figure 5) and they paid little attention to the economic organization of local villages and the Inca state. Unlike the sailors who accompanied Christopher Columbus to the Caribbean in 1492, the invaders rarely bartered with ordinary Andean people, and their uncompensated seizure of staple goods and human labor was so rapacious that Inca men later described them as "lordless plunderers" (*quitas pumarangra*) who might signal the end of the world (Betanzos 1996[1550s, part I, chapter 20]).

After the Spaniards pillaged the wealth of Andean palaces, temples, and elite tombs, they turned to staple economies to enrich settlers and fund colonial government and Catholic conversion efforts (Figure 6). The reign of Philip II (1556–1598) saw the establishment of commodity markets, coinage, wage labor, and land sales in colonial Peru – developments that heralded the spreading transatlantic networks of the mercantilist era. Even as a crown prince, Philip expressed interest in how Inca precedent could define his sovereign control over land, labor, and resources in the Andes. He sent questionnaires to prominent Spaniards in Peru during the early 1550s, inquiring about the ownership of lands and herds, as well as the labor and goods that supported the Inca and his provincial officials (Philip II [1553], in Santillán 1879[1563]). By treating Inca practices as a sovereign precedent for his own policies, Philip claimed that his demands were sustainable and relatively moderate, an ideological

Figure 5 A 1597 Dutch portrayal of the delivery of treasure for Atahualpa's ransom. Courtesy of John Carter Brown Library.

position intended to counter Protestant criticism over the devastating impact of colonization on Andean populations. Such claims attempted to obscure the fact that enslavement, overwork, and disease contributed to significant Indigenous population declines during the 1500s, especially in coastal regions.

Among those responding to Philip's questionnaire were Fernando de Santillán, a royal judge in Lima, and Polo de Ondegardo, who served as a municipal official in Cuzco. Both agreed that the Incas imposed a tripartite division of lands and herds – royal, religious, and local – in conquered provinces, but their accounts of local tribute practices differed. Focusing on the coast, Santillán stated that Inca subjects paid tribute in kind from what they produced – farmers gave local crops, fishers gave fish, and weavers gave cloth. He noted that barter was sometimes involved in tributary practices, such as if an official in charge of weavers needed to trade lowland products like chili peppers with neighboring groups for wool. Santillán said that some tribute goods were transported to Cuzco, while others were stored locally in Inca storehouses. Inca service included gold and silver mining, and those tributes were paid in metal sheets (*chipanas*), which were taken to Cuzco along with all colorful featherwork and fine cloth that artisans produced.

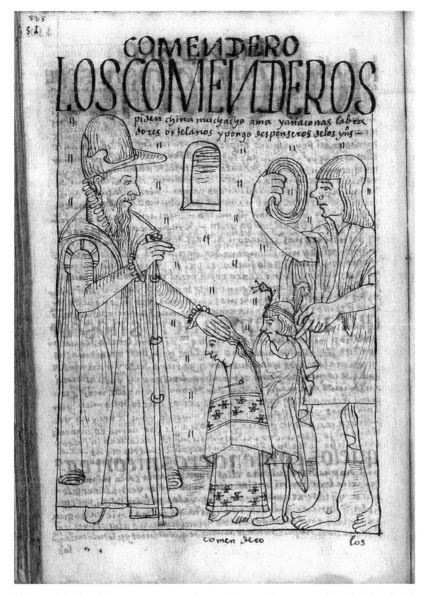

Figure 6 A Spanish *encomendero* demands unpaid servants for his household. Guaman Poma de Ayala, *El primer nueva corónica [y buen gobierno conpuesto por Don Phelipe Guaman Poma de Ayala, señor y príncipe]* (c. 1615), GKS 2232 folio, Royal Danish Library, p. 551[565]/drawing 223.

By contrast, Ondegardo's highland account stated that Inca tribute consisted only of labor. He described Inca subjects as peasant farmers who were allocated only enough land to feed themselves and were permitted only to possess the things needed for basic human subsistence. His description of the Inca tripartite system claimed that there was no private property, nor the means of acquiring it, and that people did not barter or engage in other economic transactions. Ondegardo (1940[1561]:144–145) claimed that "in the time of the Incas it is certain that they had no respect for money [i.e. coinage] in any form, because they did not buy food with gold or silver." He noted, however, that coastal people formerly carried goods into the highlands to trade for gold and silver, a practice that was common before Inca conquest, but disappeared after the Incas expanded into the lowlands and sought to monopolize the flow of precious metals and fine craft goods. Together, Santillán and Ondegardo describe regional differences in Inca-era economies. Other early chroniclers identified a highland political economy that mobilized labor to produce surpluses for state use, monopolizing exotic materials and wealth goods for the exclusive use of the Inca nobility and the state religion. Descriptions of coastal economies indicated greater specialization and exchange, including the presence of artisans and traders who did not produce their own food.

The early descriptions of Inca-era land tenure and labor tribute were written with a purpose: to help intensify Spanish colonial practices that already emphasized corporate landholding and labor service. When Philip sent his economic questionnaire to Peru, tributary populations there were administered as *encomiendas*, which were theoretically spiritual trusteeships whereby a Spaniard provided Catholic doctrine to Indigenous *caciques* and their subjects, who in turn produced food from their own lands and provided labor for the *encomendero*'s household. The Spanish Crown considered the tribute and labor delivered to the *encomendero* as services that Indigenous vassals owed to their sovereign – a feudalistic arrangement that treated Indigenous lands as collectively held and inalienable. Annual tribute levies (*tasas*) that specified the categories and amounts of tribute in kind (e.g., maize, eggs, charcoal) appeared around 1550. Although Spanish writers played up the absence of coinage in the Inca world, it was only in the mid-1560s that the first coins were minted in Peru and Europeans living in the Andes began to move away from a barter-based economy themselves.

Inca Economics under Colonial Rule

Almost twenty years after Philip II first solicited descriptions of Inca political economy, he sent a new viceroy to Peru to intensify royal administration. Francisco de Toledo arrived in 1569 and substantially altered the economic relationship between the Indigenous population and the developing mercantilism of the "Spanish republic" (Merluzzi 2003). Viewing Inca precedents as an impediment to direct Crown administration, Toledo resettled Andean communities into concentrated Spanish-style towns and advocated for the reallocation of their communal farmlands and pastures. After conducting a census of tributary populations, he announced new *tasas* that focused on a limited set of staple commodities (e.g., maize, wheat, potatoes, camelids), as well as payments in silver. Most staple goods were expected to be produced locally on community lands, whereas silver could be obtained through wage labor or by selling surplus goods. Most Europeans living in the Andes did not hold an *encomienda* grant, and Toledo channeled low-wage labor to their economic enterprises by modifying Andean cyclical labor practices. He permitted Spaniards to maintain full-time agrarian laborers called *yanaconas* (the name given to royal Inca servants) and required tributary communities to make regular rotations of workers available for hire (*mita*), many of them forced to work in distant silver and mercury mines. In the short term, the new labor practices generated significant revenues for the Spanish Crown. Tribute payments increased, commodity markets generated new taxes, and Andean mines produced hundreds of tons of assayed silver annually, which was shipped to Spain and minted into coins to pay Philip's mounting sovereign debts.

By the early 1600s, however, colonial economic demands had worsened Indigenous population declines and stimulated the flight of tributary workers, some of whom migrated toward wage labor arrangements in Spanish cities and on private rural lands (*haciendas*). Around that time, men of Andean heritage began to write about the Inca economy, a system that they had never witnessed first-hand. Guaman Poma, whose illustration opened this *Element*, described how Inca labor tribute had once filled storehouses and produced artisan goods for the palace. The Inca Garcilaso de la Vega, son of a *conquistador* and an Inca princess, published an account of Inca economics in his 1609 chronicle, which focused on the state intensification of maize farming through the construction of new terraces and irrigation works. Garcilaso de la Vega clarified earlier claims of widespread Inca appropriation of local lands, arguing that the tripartite division mentioned by earlier writers occurred *after* improvements were made, providing subjects with more land than they required to meet their basic needs. He said that there was limited occupational specialization in rural villages, and that households produced their own clothing and tools. Although Guaman Poma mentioned barter markets (*cato*) in Inca cities, Garcilaso de la Vega wrote that provincial trade only occurred in these places during state-organized festivals.

Garcilaso de la Vega described a labor-based tribute system, but he also stated that Inca subjects wove cloth for the military as a tributary service. He claimed that wealth goods were not given as tribute, and they were not valued as "treasure" since the Incas did not use gold and silver for buying and selling goods. Instead, Inca subjects supposedly offered such things to the Inca ruler as gifts when they came into possession of them. Garcilaso de la Vega's portrayal of the Inca political economy contrasted with the mercantilist practices of colonial Peru, stressing local self-sufficiency, the use of labor tribute for economic intensification, and the restricted use of wealth as an expression of royal generosity. Because the chronicle was widely printed and translated, it influenced European perceptions of the Inca economy well into the nineteenth century.

Inca Economics and the Social Sciences

In the waning years of Spanish colonial rule in the Americas, new economic theories cast the pre-contact Andes as less evolved than the mercantilist networks that paved the way for global capitalism. When Adam Smith published *The Wealth of Nations* in 1776, he devoted little attention to Indigenous economics, which he placed behind Western societies in an evolutionary sequence based on subsistence practices and trade. Smith viewed Native Americans as technologically backward for their lack of draft animals and iron, noting (Smith 1776:book IV, chapter 7) that they "had no coined money, nor any established instrument of commerce of any kind." He designated the Incas as a barter-based economy belonging to the "Age of Agriculture," rather than his most advanced stage of human attainment, the "Age of Commerce." This depiction of the Incas reflected changing economic practices in Europe and was consistent with Enlightenment-era descriptions of the Americas as uncivilized and of Indigenous populations as racially inferior.

When the American writer William Prescott (1847:I:41) published the first modern history of the conquest of Peru in 1847, he echoed Smith's attitude about Native American economies. The Incas were "a people who had no money, little trade, and hardly any thing [*sic*] that could be called fixed property," possessing instead a rudimentary barter economy and a political economy based on labor. Prescott's (1847:I:56) principal criticism of the pre-capitalist Inca economy was that it offered no incentive for individual innovation and advancement: "The Peruvian, laboring all his life for others, might be compared to the convict in a treadmill, going the same dull round of incessant toil, with the consciousness, that, however profitable the results to the state, they were nothing to him. But this is the dark side of the picture. If no man could become rich in Peru, no man could become poor."

Karl Marx and Friedrich Engels, who were writing *The Communist Manifesto* when Prescott's history was published, embraced the virtues of poverty eradication through a state-administered economy that limited personal property. At the same time, their grand historical progression – from primitive communism to capitalism – treated barter-based economies like those of the Andes as less developed because they did not recognize private property that could be alienated. In *Das Kapital*, Marx (1906:100) argued that "such a state of reciprocal independence has no existence in a primitive society based on property in common, whether such a society takes the form of a patriarchal family, an ancient Indian community, or a Peruvian Inca state." Rather than an alternative to market economies, Marx characterized the Inca Empire as economically underdeveloped, a network of kin-based communities rather than a civil society. His intellectual successors and critics were of two minds about this interpretation. Some viewed the empire as a despotic socialist state that absolutely controlled its subjects, suppressing their individual development and free enterprise. Others, such as the German theorist Heinrich Cunow, argued that the socialistic attributes of the Inca Empire came not from state policies, but from the coalescence of extended kin groups (*ayllus*) that developed before the Incas and managed themselves using "primitive" economic principles.

Even after the Russian Revolution, Inca economics provided fodder for political debates over socialism in modern nation-states. José Carlos Mariátegui, a founder of Peru's Communist Party, argued that Inca socialism should be the basis for governing highland populations in modern Peru. Leading Peruvian archaeologists shared this vision of the past. Julio C. Tello, (1952:25), a founding father of Peruvian archaeology, praised the "miraculous" impact of Inca socialism, which focused on transforming every Inca man "into a dynamic factor, oriented toward the domination of Nature, toward the exploitation of the riches of the soil, by means of intense and tenacious cooperative labor." Those opposed to the spread of communism sometimes characterized the Inca Empire as a nanny state that exercised so much control over individual lives that Inca people were unable to resist Pizarro and his handful of Spaniards after Atahualpa was captured. Whether praising or criticizing Inca "socialism," these studies did not take a comprehensive view of the diverse Andean world. They also denied the rational self-interest of individual Andean people, as well as the conditions of scarcity that would motivate strategic decision-making.

Anthropology and the Incas

After World War II, several US-based anthropologists became prominent in Inca studies, introducing new approaches to Andean economies. John Murra (1956) advocated a substantivist interpretation of economic life, which emphasized social relationships over individual self-interest, and reciprocity and redistribution over market exchange. Critical of previous work that foregrounded the despotic welfare policies of the Inca state, Murra focused instead on the "peasant economies" of ordinary farmers and herders. He treated Inca political economy as an extrapolation of kin groups (*ayllus*) that were organized around principles of reciprocity (*ayni*) and economic self-sufficiency. Murra argued that highland *ayllus* settled and worked across diverse ecozones to exploit a broad range of resources directly, a regional phenomenon that he initially called a "vertical archipelago" (scholars today refer to such practices as *ecological complementarity*). Inca imperial rule built on the foundations of highland *ayllu* economies, establishing new social statuses and productive resources tied to the ruler.

Murra noted that a model based on the economic practices of small highland communities was not necessarily a good fit for studying pre-Inca societies or lowland populations, which maintained long-distance exchange networks that were largely independent from Inca administration (Murra 2017[1969]:21, 47–49). Some of this nuance was lost as a new generation of Andeanist scholars began to apply Murra's *ayllu*-oriented approach to their research in the late 1960s and after. Many anthropologists at this time pursued a synthesis of colonial ethnohistory, archaeology, and ethnographic description, describing distinctive Andean features that they thought were widespread and enduring (Figure 7). Ethnographers and ethnohistorians focused on local *ayllus*, debating how those groups used *ayni* to maintain networks of ecological complementarity. These were seen as central building blocks for understanding Inca and pre-Inca economic practices, although archaeologists and anthropologists soon raised questions about their pre-Inca time depth in certain regions (Mayer 2002; Stanish 1989) and identified evidence for markets and bartering in some parts of the ancient Andes (Hirth and Pillsbury 2013).

Despite these issues, archaeologists studying the late prehispanic Andes have generally accepted the *ayllu*-based model of local economic organization, partly because the scale of archaeological investigation is rarely well suited to identifying the subtle material culture patterns needed to test the model within communities, or across ecologically diverse regions. Excavations and surveys have nevertheless contributed valuable perspectives on the economic lives of individuals and households, revealing more subsistence variation and economic inequality than an idealized *ayllu* model anticipates. At a regional level, archaeologists have developed a diverse array of local case studies describing the negotiation of Inca economic policies. Such work treats imperial political economy as a set of policies that had to be tailored to local conditions, rather than a form of statecraft extending naturally from the cultural logic of local *ayllus*.

Figure 7 Many researchers in the late twentieth century combined the observations of early colonial writers like Guaman Poma de Ayala with archaeology and ethnography to describe highland kin-based economies. Guaman Poma de Ayala c. 1615, GKS 2232 folio, Royal Danish Library, p. 1147[1157]/drawing 391.

Archaeology offers long-term perspectives on local subsistence practices, social organization, and economic inequality in different regions, and how they changed under Inca rule. Understanding local pre-Inca economies makes it

possible to reconstruct aspects of the dynamic layering of Inca political economy onto diverse existing practices, to consider how new forms of production
and distribution amplified (and altered) local networks, without necessarily
displacing them. Kenneth Hirth and Joanne Pillsbury (2013:645) refer to this
as *economic plasticity*, an interpretive framing that generates new questions
about the degree of economic growth in different contexts, who benefited
from it, and how new resources were distributed and consumed. The remaining
sections of this *Element* explore the interplay between political, regional,
and domestic economies in different social and ecological contexts, considering
how local populations navigated their roles in an empire that was still
growing and consolidating at the time of its violent collision with the early
modern West.

3 The "Noble Economy" of Cuzco

We begin in Cuzco, where economic growth primarily occurred through elite
projects that improved fertile farmlands and stimulated wealth production at
the heart of the empire. Descendants of the ruling dynasty – rather than
functionaries representing state institutions – controlled the "noble economy"
and extended it amidst existing networks of local farmers and herders.
Spaniards who settled in Cuzco for precious metals, productive farmlands,
and abundant labor learned from Inca noblemen that the royal domain traced
back generations, perhaps to the time of Manco Capac, the first Inca. Spanish
colonization interrupted a dynastic project that built imperial power by producing and consuming vast staple and wealth resources in social performances
intended to glorify the ruling family and strengthen its political alliances and
supernatural connections.

On April 23, 1555, a group of Spaniards gathered on a plot of fallow land in the
fertile Vilcanota Valley, just to the north of Cuzco (Figure 8). Martín de Meneses,
a wealthy *encomendero*, sought to acquire the lands, which supposedly had been
abandoned for more than twenty-five years. Don Diego Ataurimache, an Inca
nobleman from the nearby town of Calca, contested the Spaniard's claim, stating
that his people had held use rights there since Inca times. To prove that the lands
were exclusively Inca property – and not available to Ataurimache and local
farmers – Meneses presented caciques from other villages. One testified that the
disputed field was a gravelly riverbed until Huascar, the last pre-conquest Inca,
sent provincial laborers to shift the river's course and construct irrigated valley-
bottom terraces. Huascar named the new fields Pomabamba (Puma Plain), and
claimed the maize harvested from the new terraces for his exclusive use in Cuzco.
Ataurimache disagreed with this account, insisting that the Inca allowed the

Figure 8 The Vilcamayu (Vilcanota–Urubamba) Valley near Calca.

people of Calca to farm some of the new terraces – a common claim that local villagers made in other early colonial lawsuits. The Spanish judge sided with Meneses, granting him a small piece of the royal landscape that Inca rulers had been building in the Cuzco region for more than two centuries (Rostworowski 1993[1555]:118–119).

Inca Expansion History and Estates

Huascar created the lands of Pomabamba just before his war with Atahualpa, which ended in his capture and execution in 1532. Although his reign was brief, Huascar also managed to build a country palace at Calca and a lakeside villa at Kañaraqay. These projects represent the culmination of roughly seven generations of royal Inca landscape development, which transformed rural Cuzco into the wealthy heartland of a mighty empire (Quave 2018). Beginning with Inca Rocca, the sixth Inca, royal couples used labor services owed to them by their kin and subjects to construct irrigation canals, terraces, corrals, and country palaces (Figure 9). These new properties belonged to the Inca and *Coya* (empress) who built them, and after their deaths their mummies remained the owners of the resources that maintained the noble house (*panaca*) made up of their descendants. Early estate projects were modest undertakings, begun as Inca elites built alliances and political power among the small farming and herding groups living near Cuzco. Inca Rocca and his wife, Mama Micay, developed terraces at Larapa, on the north side of the Cuzco Basin, and they

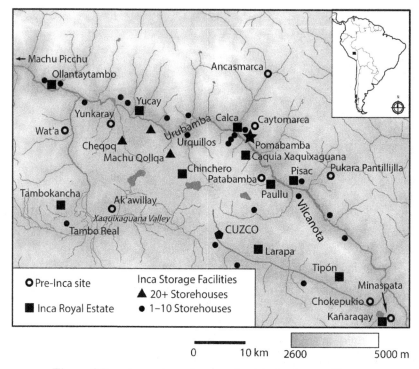

Figure 9 Royal country palaces and estate lands near Cuzco.

commissioned the Chacán canal, which supported urban growth in the upper (*hanan*) part of Cuzco. Their son, Yahuar Huaccac, constructed valley-bottom lodgings and farmland at Paullu in the Vilcanota Valley (known today as the Sacred Valley), close to Patabamba, the hilltop town where his mother's kin lived (Covey 2006).

As Inca imperial growth intensified, rulers completed multiple estate projects in the valleys surrounding Cuzco. After defeating the people of Huaiparmarca, Viracocha Inca built a country palace at Tipón (LaLone and LaLone 1987), and he made the conquered population of Caytomarca build him palaces at Calca and Caquia Xaquixaguana (Juchuy Qosqo) in the Sacred Valley. His son, the famous Pachacuti Inca Yupanqui, also developed impressive palaces in that valley, at Pisac, Ollantaytambo, and Machu Picchu. Famous for their innovative architecture, fine stonework, and arresting landscape design, these country estates also included major investments to canalize meandering rivers and construct irrigated complexes of valley-bottom fields and terraces.

Later rulers faced increasing labor requirements and logistical considerations to complete land improvement projects that would establish their own *panacas* in the

Sacred Valley. Topa Inca Yupanqui and Mama Ocllo chose to build their country palace at Chinchero, on a high, chilly plain located more than 800 meters above their valley-bottom fields at Urquillos, where they improved almost 100 hectares of frost-free lands. They also constructed a palace at Tambokancha in the marshy Xaquixaguana Valley, and another in the Amaybamba Valley, close to new coca plantations (Quave 2018). Huayna Capac, Huascar's father, built just one estate, in the Yucay area of the Sacred Valley, a monumental reshaping of the valley that reportedly involved 150,000 provincial workers (Figure 10). After surveying the Cuzco region to find wild and unoccupied lands, the Inca summoned tributary laborers to transform the valley for him.

> He had the river moved ... making it stronger and making a bed where it went. Along the path of the river the Inca had hills leveled. Thus he made the valley flat so that it could be planted and harvested. There he had houses built and lodgings where he could go to enjoy himself. In this valley he gave farmlands to the lords of Cuzco, both to the living and to the dead lords whose statues were there. They sent their young *yanacona* servants to cultivate their vegetables and other things for their enjoyment. There Huayna Capac had many small towns of twenty, thirty, and fifty Indians built. In these towns he put many *mitimae* [labor colonist] Indians from all the nations and provinces of the land (Betanzos 1996[1550s:170, part I chapter 43]).

Figure 10 Valley-bottom lands of Huayna Capac in the Yucay Valley.

Despite the Inca claim to have civilized uninhabited spaces, there were in fact few arable lands in the Cuzco region that were unoccupied by the early sixteenth century. In the Yucay Valley, archaeological surveys have recorded dozens of pre-Inca settlements in the valley-bottom lands where Huayna Capac built his estate, and excavations at Pisac and Ollantaytambo have encountered evidence of earlier occupations beneath Pachacuti's country palaces (Covey 2018). Competition over improved (or improvable) lands came to a head during Huascar's brief reign. Although he emulated his ancestors in constructing new lands and palaces near Cuzco, Huascar also complained bitterly that the mummies of his predecessors possessed the best resources, even though they had no need to eat. In one account, he declared his intent to confiscate the lands of the noble *panacas*, a decision that would have overturned generations of noble wealth-building in the imperial heartland (Betanzos 1996[1550s]). The Inca civil war and European invasion prevented him from realizing this plan.

Rural Landscape Development

Inca estate construction created economic resources through performances celebrating sovereign power. The Inca and Coya acted as founding ancestors who occupied wild landscapes, using the labor of their subjects to civilize and settle them. Estate projects manipulated Andean origin myths, where creators raised up the mountains, made the waters flow in their courses, and sent the first people to the places where they would emerge and settle. The Inca and Coya converted rock outcrops into masonry, flattened hills and gullies, and diverted rushing streams into irrigation canals. After creating these new landscapes, they peopled them with small communities of *yanacona*, former adversaries who became servants of the royal house. Estate construction demonstrated Inca "wealth in people" while also marking rural landscapes near Cuzco as civilized royal properties (Figure 11).

By the time Inca rulers began to build country palaces, agricultural villages had existed in the Cuzco region for two millennia. The region's environmental diversity inspired people to establish communities from the floors of the major valleys (around 2,900 meters above sea level) to prominent hilltops (up to 4,200 meters) overlooking the high pastures where llamas and alpacas grazed. People experimented with different combinations of Andean crops – maize, potatoes, quinoa, beans, and other plants – and social relationships that would reduce the risks of crop failure and food shortages. Over time, environmental fluctuations and social disruptions contributed to the abandonment of many of the earliest villages, but in a few places, communities persisted in the face of significant

Figure 11 Inca agricultural terracing at Urquillos in the Sacred Valley.

changes. Valley-bottom sites such as Chokepukio, Ak'awillay, and Minaspata show evidence of ongoing habitation as many upland settlements faded, and they continued to thrive after maize-farming colonists affiliated with the Wari empire settled in the area to the southeast of Cuzco. The centuries of Wari colonization (AD 600–1000) left a mark on the Lucre Basin and Huaro area, where the unfinished administrative center of Pikillacta was under construction (Figure 12), but they had less impact elsewhere in the Cuzco region, where small villages of farmers maintained their valley-bottom fields and many of the cultural practices that had defined them before the arrival of the outsiders (Covey et al. 2013).

Around AD 1000, social unrest and climatic fluctuations, including extended droughts, encouraged populations across the Andean highlands to abandon the intensive agricultural practices that supported the Wari state and its highland rival, Tiwanaku. Local kin networks and communities shifted their food-producing strategies away from irrigation networks and raised fields, adapting to riskier times by incorporating camelid herding and cultivating a diverse array of dry-farmed crops. Across the central highlands, people moved to new locations that offered local access to a range of microenvironments, often selecting sites with natural defenses against raids that could deprive them of herd animals, food stores, and community members. Such developments, which receive more attention in Section 4, occurred in some parts of the Cuzco region, especially in the uplands overlooking the Sacred Valley and the margins of the Cuzco Valley.

Figure 12 The Wari site of Pikillacta, with Chokepukio in the background.
Shippee-Johnson Expedition, Courtesy of the American Museum of Natural
History Library (AMNH), Asset ID: 334819.

In those areas, modest villages like Pukara Pantillijlla, Ancasmarca, and Wat'a
occupied prominent ridgetops at the ecological transition between hillside
farmlands and high pastures (Covey 2018) (Figure 13). Their populations,
which probably numbered in the hundreds, consisted of farmers and herders
who made most of their own pottery and tools, and who lacked strong evidence
for pronounced social hierarchies or extensive participation in the production
and regional exchange of status goods.

At Pukara Pantillijlla, for example, the largest houses were single-room
structures of about 30–50 m², built on small, irregularly shaped terraces that
clung to the steep sides of a prominent ridge. Some houses had small outbuild-
ings that were probably used to store household goods. The site lacked walls or
other community defenses, and the largest "public" building was a well-built
square structure whose interior measured less than 100 m², which opened onto
a small plaza that could comfortably hold a few hundred people. The people at
Pukara Pantillijlla belonged to a group called the Cuyos, who distinguished
themselves from the neighboring Poques and Huayllacans, whose fields and
ridgetop villages were visible from the lands where they farmed and herded.
Cuyo households acquired some of their decorated pottery from neighboring
valleys, but they possessed few goods that were not locally made, and their own

Figure 13 Pukara Pantillijlla, a ridgetop village with early Inca associations.

craft goods show no evidence of specialized or large-scale production (Covey 2015).

The Incas claimed that their ancestors first emerged in the rural uplands, but chose not to remain there. Instead, they migrated to the Cuzco Basin, settling near valley-bottom lands where deep and fertile soils would produce rich maize harvests. Archaeological surveys confirm that Cuzco Basin populations had long favored the alluvial terraces just above the valley floor (Bauer 2004). Unlike most other groups in the central highlands, they did not abandon those productive lands 1000 years ago when other populations shifted to high-elevation locations. Instead, Cuzco Basin populations grew larger and more hierarchical, and hundreds of settlements flourished there during the centuries before imperial expansion. Valley-bottom settlements also thrived in a few neighboring areas, such as the Lucre Basin and the Maras district, but the Cuzco Basin had a significantly larger population. The Incas and their strongest rivals focused on intensive maize agriculture, which supported social hierarchies whose leaders could use surpluses to construct infrastructure or monuments, to support artisans, and to engage in regional alliance-building and war.

Cuzco Basin populations were more populous and better-organized than their highland neighbors, but they were not exactly wealthy or powerful – certainly not by the standards of coastal rulers of that time, who were buried in monumental tombs filled with precious metals and fine craft goods. Compared with Wari and Inca state constructions, the most elaborate surviving pre-imperial architecture is modest, as seen in the walled enclosures and single-room temples that Gordon McEwan and Arminda Gibaja excavated at Chokepukio (McEwan et al. 2005). At Yunkaray, another valley-bottom center that resisted Inca incorporation, Kylie Quave and her colleagues excavated high percentages of locally made decorated pottery, but encountered almost no regional trade goods, such as metal or shell (Quave et al. 2018). In their early centuries of expansion, Inca leaders in the Cuzco Basin emphasized wealth not by accumulating and flaunting personal adornments, but by building relationships and investing the labor of kin and allies – and eventually, subjects – to carry out acts of landscape transformation. Stonework was a durable and visible expression of Inca wealth and power, and the construction of new valley-bottom farming landscapes had long-term economic implications as the Incas eclipsed local rivals and began to conquer beyond the Cuzco region.

New Identities

Advancing a risk-management strategy distinct from that of hillside farmers and high-elevation herders, Inca rulers transformed river valleys surrounding Cuzco into an engineered landscape. Intensive valley-bottom agriculture emphasized surplus production over diversity, and the royal patrons who organized the construction of irrigated lands also controlled land tenure and staple surpluses that could be used in a variety of ways. In a bad year, Inca stores could feed subjects during the lean months and provide seeds for the next planting. Conversely, good harvests financed lavish feasts that reciprocated tributary labor and fed workers as they built new terraces and road infrastructure and raised Cuzco's impressive palaces and temples. By strategically pressing their subjects harder for a season or two, Inca rulers could also amass supplies needed to mobilize large armies for campaigns beyond the Cuzco region, where they overwhelmed local highland populations.

Construction projects extended sovereign control into the diverse landscapes of rural Cuzco, and they were associated with the resettlement of resistant groups. Inca men recounted the forcible resettlement of the Pinaguas and Ayarmacas, who lived at the valley-bottom centers of Chokepukio and Yunkaray (Espinoza Soriano 1974; Rostworowski 1970). They claimed that the Cuyos and other groups were eliminated after conspiring against the Inca (Covey 2006). Although colonial accounts should be read cautiously, imperial-era settlement patterns indicate widespread settlement disruption in many parts of the Cuzco region (Covey 2018). In the upper valleys, where mixed rainfall farming and herding sustained modest ridgetop villages, Inca-era settlement shifted toward valley-bottom areas where royal intensification projects developed new irrigated farmland. There was more settlement continuity in places where local populations were already farming maize (e.g., Bauer 1992; Bauer et al. 2022), although some areas experienced widespread site abandonment when Inca rulers appropriated lands for estate projects or religious purposes.

Inca descriptions of the earliest land improvement projects in the Cuzco Basin say that local leaders from the surrounding region brought their people to the valley to work for the Inca nobility (Betanzos 1996 [1550s]). As the empire grew, rulers summoned tens of thousands of *mitimaes* and tributary laborers from far-flung provinces to build their palaces and country estates. Although the *mitimaes* theoretically resided in Cuzco temporarily, the large population designated as *yanaconas* and *mamaconas* did not return to their homelands, and DNA evidence from burials at Machu Picchu indicates a cosmopolitan community drawn from across the Inca realm (Salazar et al. 2023). The genetic evidence complements colonial household surveys from Huayna Capac's Yucay estate, where the *yanacona* population represented nearly fifty different groups, including large numbers from resistant frontier groups like the Chachapoyas and Cañaris (Covey and Amado 2008).

Throughout the Inca heartland, warm valley-bottom areas were developed for irrigation agriculture, and parts of rural Cuzco experienced population growth rates that suggest influxes of resettled population and other migrants. Within the Cuzco Basin, new villages and hamlets sprang up, increasing the count of rural sites by more than 300% during the imperial period (Bauer 2004). Some new settlements were Inca-planned, but others grew opportunistically at the edges of already-occupied lands. Inca-era site counts also increased near the floor of the Sacred Valley and the outer basins of the Cuzco Valley, and on the hillside farming landscapes of Paruro to the south (Bauer 1992; Bauer et al. 2022; Covey 2014). Population pressures in the Cuzco Basin might have stimulated some of the elite-sponsored land improvement projects in the surrounding valleys – early colonial records identify at least five nearby towns (Lamay, Coya, Pisac, Calca, Zurite) that had *ayllus* that identified as originally coming from Cuzco (Covey 2006).

The rural populations that labored directly for the Inca nobility and the state religion produced unprecedented surplus staples, which were preserved at storage depots built across rural Cuzco, such as Cheqoq and Machu Qollqa (Covey et al. 2016; Quave 2012) (Figure 14). Some of that bounty supported the luxuries of palace life and provided the food and drink served at public spectacles in Cuzco.

Figure 14 Storage structures at Ollantaytambo, a site associated with the estate of Pachacuti Inca Yupanqui. Storehouses near Cuzco are architecturally distinct from the *collcas* seen along Inca provincial roads.

Rural farmlands also fed Inca priestesses, lower-order officials, and the artisans (*camayos*) who transformed exotic raw materials into objects that distinguished the Inca nobility and bound them to powerful supernatural beings (*huacas*). Excavations in rural communities indicate that very little of the wealth produced in Cuzco trickled down to ordinary farmers and herders living nearby (e.g., Quave and Covey 2015). Inca-affiliated settlements had greater access to the decorated polychrome pottery used in state festivities (Delgado González 2014; Quave 2017), but gold and silver artifacts are rarely found in rural households, where there is also little marine shell or other evidence of regular participation in interregional exchange networks. A greater sample of lower-status households still needs to be excavated, but the available evidence suggests that many families living near Cuzco gained access to some high-quality farmlands and received Inca food and drink while providing labor service to the ruling elite. The distribution of Inca-controlled staple goods was not matched by royal gifts of wealth, and ordinary people did not participate regularly in long-distance trade.

The limited wealth circulating among non-noble populations in the Inca heartland is also reflected in burial practices, which deployed fewer resources in tomb construction and grave goods than can be observed for contemporary coastal societies (see Section 5). At Sacsayhuaman, a group of thirteen elite burials yielded almost ninety pieces of Inca-style pottery, but other goods were surprisingly rare. Marine shell appeared in just four burials, and the thirty-four metal artifacts from the assemblage consisted mostly of women's shawl pins (n=twenty), which were mostly made of copper, bronze, and lead. Only eight silver artifacts were present, and there was no gold reported (Julien 1987). Mortuary inventories from Machu Picchu (Gordon and Knopf 2007) and other sites near Cuzco (Flammang 2021) also indicate only modest amounts of metal, with limited quantities of silver and almost no gold. Most burials lack substantial investment in tomb architecture. Aside from the Inca nobility, whose mummies circulated in the imperial capital and possessed palaces and farmlands, most people in the Cuzco region did not channel significant resources into elaborate funerary displays or grave offerings.

Storage and Royal Reciprocity

The modest household and funerary contexts encountered by archaeologists in rural Cuzco contrast sharply with the dazzling accounts of the imperial capital written by the first Spaniards. The *conquistador* Pedro Sancho (1968[1534: chapter 17]) described a city filled with finely built palaces and orderly blocks of houses made of masonry and adobe. In the "fortress" of Sacsayhuaman, he found stores of weaponry and military garb collected from Inca provinces, as well as raw materials for making fancy craft goods. Sancho recalled that "[t]hey had many pigments – blues, yellows, blacks, and many others – for dyeing cloths; and a great deal of tin and lead [for making bronze] with other metals, and lots of silver and some gold." From the walls of Sacsayhuaman, Sancho surveyed the surrounding valley, which contained country estates of the Inca *panacas* and tens of thousands of houses. Rows of long storehouses lined the hillsides, and many were still stocked with wool, textiles, weapons, and an array of craft goods (Bauer 2004). Some held construction materials, household implements, and tribute that people brought to their lords. Sancho entered one storehouse packed with the bodies of Amazonian birds – he estimated that there were 100,000 of them – whose colorful feathers would be worked into elaborate garments or woven onto the stately litters that carried Inca lords and powerful sacred objects. Even after Spaniards plundered Cuzco for Atahualpa's ransom, the city's palaces, temples, and royal tombs continued to surrender gold, silver, and precious stones to the invaders.

Cuzco's concentration of stored goods and displayed wealth reflected Inca efforts to make their capital into a center where exotic materials would be transformed into materials fine enough to be used by Inca royalty or offered as sacrifices. According to Juan de Betanzos (1996[1550s]), the storage infra-structure of the Cuzco region developed over several generations, beginning in the early years of Pachacuti Inca Yupanqui's reign. The first storehouses were built to hold food, tools, and other things needed to provision work crews and Inca armies on campaign, whereas later projects constructed facilities for the supplies necessary to provision the urban population of Cuzco. There were also storehouses that held foodstuffs and goods belonging to the Inca nobility and religious institutions. The *mestizo* chronicler Garcilaso de la Vega (1609) recalled that these were still in use during the 1550s, with different groups maintaining their own bins (*pirhua*) inside the long, rectangular structures built throughout the capital region.

Inca rulers resettled *camayo* households, such as silversmiths, to their capital to fabricate fine craft goods with the exotic materials that flowed there. Artisans produced wealth goods for the use of the royal family – including occasional gifts presented to distinguished subjects – as well as for religious offerings to supernatural entities (*huacas*) that sustained the universe and influenced the conditions necessary for human life. Powerful Inca women, including the Coya and the *mamacona* priestesses, maintained kin relationships with the Sun, the Moon, the Thunder, and other beings, providing them special food, drink, and clothing. Inca rulers and the nobility also made wealth offerings during annual observations that marked their ceremonial calendar. They buried gold and silver figurines, scattered marine shells, and periodically burned hundreds of llamas from Inca herds (see Delgado González 2013). In times of crisis, the Inca ruler presided over the *capacocha* ritual, sanctifying pairs of boys and girls in Cuzco's central plaza before sending them out as human sacrifices to prominent mountains and other powerful sacred places.

The sacrifices dispatched from Cuzco reflected the rare outward flow of Inca wealth goods. Inca policies limited the non-religious movement of most wealth produced in the capital. According to Pedro de Cieza de León (1984[1553: chapter 14]), the Incas "ordered by law that no gold or silver that entered the city of Cuzco could leave it, under penalty of death." Guards reportedly searched travelers at the major bridges leaving the Inca heartland, to ensure that they were not transporting unauthorized wealth. This surveillance attempted to distinguish the elevated status of the Incas from subjects living in the highland provinces, where "no rich person could wear more jewelry or different outfits than the poor, except for lords and *curacas*" (Cieza de León 1984[1553:chapter 19]). Based on burials excavated in the Cuzco region, these sumptuary restrictions appear to have applied to all but the highest-ranking Inca men and women, and dampened any non-royal demand for exotic raw materials and fine craft goods in the highlands.

The wealth economy of Inca Cuzco was not based on transactions, and thus did not rely on markets, although Pachacuti reportedly established a barter market (*cato*) early in his reign, which probably focused on exchanges of staple goods (Betanzos 1996[1550s:part 1, chapter 21]). Wealth goods produced in the Cuzco region were not used to transform staple surpluses into concentrated and portable exchange media that could be used in interregional financial transactions. What we think of as wealth largely circulated through a royal gift economy that emphasized values of kinship and reciprocity. Inca royals used their sovereign right to labor to improve farmlands and build palaces, and they reciprocated that labor symbolically by providing food and tools for laborers, and underwriting feasts to celebrate the successful completion of work. In turn, the Incas used improved lands and surplus goods to put certain women and men to work perfecting their skills in different artisan tasks, providing them with lands, housing, and necessary supplies. The most powerful Inca nobles increased their wealth, but they disposed of many of the finest goods produced in the empire ceremonially, as generous offerings to the ancestral dead (whose palaces and lands they enjoyed) and to supernatural beings that sustained the universe that the Incas dominated.

Conclusions

The economy of the Inca imperial heartland used the fiction of royal reciprocity to mobilize labor, improve lands, and work raw materials in ways that elevated the royal palace, the Inca nobility, and the capital region above the imperial provinces. The emphasis on personal relationships and obligations limited the role of economic transactions and the need for high-value objects that could finance populations not engaged in subsistence work. Other than a few religious institutions, such as the Sun temple and the *acllahuasi* cloister, the noble *panacas* controlled virtually all nonlocal resources and drove the trajectory of economic intensification and specialization in the Cuzco region. Noble factions stimulated economic growth in the imperial heartland, creating extensive dynastic resources, as well as new lands that drew rural populations into closer relationships as Inca subjects. Labor service, surplus management, and wealth production by the palace and the leading *panacas* fulfilled many of the functions of a political economy, and the beneficiaries of the noble economy acted in place of a specialized and professional civil service in the administrative work that bound Cuzco to its most intensively governed highland provinces. Such features do not correspond exactly to expectations about the political-economic organization of early states and empires, and the evidence from Cuzco makes it difficult to identify governmental institutions and bureaucrats that functioned to amplify staple production, generate taxes, and distribute state revenue in ways that reinforced state power. However, the self-dealing, nepotism, and factional competition described in Inca history were probably features of other ancient empires – they are undeniably elements of the politics and economics of the twenty-first century.

4 Inca Political Economy in the Highland Provinces

The generations of royal economic development that transformed the Cuzco region had a profound impact on the highland regions closest to the Inca capital (Figure 15). Early military campaigns and infrastructural projects bound the inner provinces to the growing empire, altering local subsistence economies and social hierarchies. The imperial state benefited from economic growth, accumulating staple goods at installations along the royal road system, and channeling exotic raw materials and finished goods to Cuzco to enhance the noble

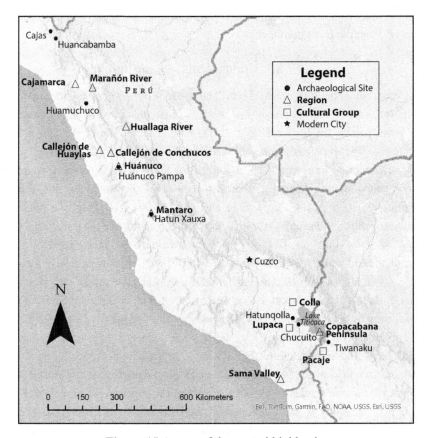

Figure 15 A map of the central highlands.

economy there. Local elites participated in, and benefited from, provincial political economies to varying degrees. A review of three highland provinces – the upper Mantaro Valley, the Huánuco region, and the Lake Titicaca Basin – describes some common threads in Inca provincial strategies, as well as the ways that ecology and existing social organization influenced the implementation of new economic practices.

In 1570, the Spanish viceroy Francisco de Toledo visited the Mantaro Valley of highland Peru to oversee the administrative reorganization of the native Wanka people (Levillier 1940[1570]:22–23). Eager to displace local *curacas* and the vestiges of Inca imperial institutions, Toledo ordered a new census and tribute levies for the population, which he commanded to resettle into gridded Iberian-style towns. To resist these changes, Wanka lords presented notarized depositions and legal papers that they had compiled over the years, which they said confirmed their existing rights and privileges. Toledo confiscated the documents and burned most of them publicly. He then assembled some minor village leaders (*principales*) and commoner men, soliciting sworn testimony that the Wanka *caciques* owed their power to Inca tyranny. For example, don Diego Lucana, an 85-year-old who supervised *mitimaes* from northern Peru and southern Ecuador, said that he had heard that the Wankas had no lords and paid no tribute before the Inca conquest. Instead, each village elected war leaders called *sincheconas* to defend against raids from neighboring communities. Francisco de Toledo used the testimony of don Diego and other Andean *curacas* to argue that the Incas were not natural lords, and that their provincial officials were a recent and illegitimate innovation that should have no special consideration in the new colonial political economy. Like other Spaniards who advocated for stronger royal control in the Andes, Toledo found it useful to treat Inca political economy not as an imperial precedent, but as a tyrannical legacy that harmed the interests of the true sovereign of the Andes: the Spanish Crown (Levillier 1940[1572]:11).

Toledo's campaign against the Wanka lords provides a useful point of departure for discussing economic changes taking place in the highland provinces closest to Cuzco. That region, which extended northwest to the valleys just beyond Cajamarca, and southeast to the Paria area in the Bolivian altiplano, was home to dozens of groups who spoke different dialects of Quechua and Aymara, as well as lesser-known languages, such as Uru and Puquina (Mannheim 1991:33–34). These populations pursued locally tailored combinations of irrigation agriculture, rain-fed horticulture, herding, and even fishing, making a living in mountain environments shaped by considerable variations in temperature, precipitation, elevation, and soil quality. Local labor practices varied accordingly, as did the prospects of sustainably producing food surpluses that might support artisans, administrators, and long-distance trade. Although Inca armies easily defeated the decentralized highland groups that rejected their threats and diplomatic overtures, it took decades for a succession of rulers to establish more intensive forms of provincial administration, which still varied in their organization and intensity at the time of the European invasion.

The Upper Mantaro Valley

The upper Mantaro Valley, home to the Wanka people, is unusually wide and flat, with vast expanses of fertile bottomlands suitable for maize cultivation. The first Spanish visitors marveled at the valley's rich farmlands and dense population, and Francisco Pizarro chose the Inca capital, Hatun Xauxa, as the location for Spain's first short-lived highland colony. The Spaniards were drawn not only to the agrarian prospects of the Mantaro Valley, but also to its well-developed Inca infrastructure – roads, bridges, waystations, and well-stocked storehouses – and its provincial capital, which could accommodate tens of thousands of imperial subjects during state festivals. The powerful Wanka lords won the *conquistadores* over by sending gifts of gold, silver, fine cloth, and food to them in Cajamarca. When the Spaniards marched on Cuzco in 1533, the Wankas provided porters and food, and they fought as allies against the Inca war of resistance that broke out a few years later (Espinoza Soriano 1971). These gifts and services were similar to what the Wanka had given the Incas since their conquest several generations earlier.

The Mantaro Valley represents something of a high-water mark in Inca highland administration, and extensive archaeological work by the Upper Mantaro Archaeological Research Project (UMARP) has reconstructed the pre-imperial and Inca-era organization, developing valuable perspectives on household economies and imperial finance (D'Altroy and Hastorf 2001). During the Late Intermediate Period (c. 1000–1400), the valley was one of the most densely settled highland regions, and its largest sites were among the most populous. Despite their valley's rich agrarian potential, pre-Inca Wanka groups prioritized security over the surpluses to be had from valley-bottom agriculture. Regional archaeology indicates that in the generations before the Inca conquest, Wanka villagers abandoned productive farmland and settled in new hilltop communities, where they built impressive stone fortifications to enhance natural defensive features. For perhaps a century, these communities invested considerable labor and resources to build new houses and protect them, while also navigating the risks and rewards of new subsistence practices and social arrangements. Diet shifted from maize, a valley-bottom crop, to foods that could be produced by herding camelids and cultivating potatoes, quinoa, and other crops on the

Figure 16 Tightly packed Wanka houses at Tunanmarca, a hilltop town settled before Inca conquest. Courtesy of Timothy Earle.

high slopes. Sites such as Tunanmarca and Hatunmarca became densely settled towns with populations of perhaps 10,000 residents packed onto the high ridges (Figure 16). Both communities grew with two discrete residential areas, perhaps representing social groups whose leaders coordinated community affairs. Beyond those spatial distinctions, the towns lacked central planning and public monuments, containing only limited open spaces for gatherings taking place outside of household patios (Figure 17).

Wanka centers were not cities in the making, and their thousands of tightly clustered houses showed only subtle material variations in status and identity (D'Altroy and Hastorf 2001). UMARP archaeologists identified differences in the size and construction of house compounds and individual grave offerings, although those were minimal compared to what is seen at nearby coastal centers. The largest Wanka house compounds were smaller than 200 m^2, containing less than 50 m^2 of roofed architecture. At the time they were occupied, the rulers of the Chimú Empire (discussed in Section 5) were commissioning new palace enclosures at their coastal capital that reached 10 hectares in size (100,000 m^2) and contained hundreds of audience rooms, storehouses, and burial platforms (Moseley and Day 1982). The most elaborate pre-imperial Wanka tombs rarely contained more than a dozen grave offerings, mostly locally produced pottery. At the coastal site of Sicán, a single shaft tomb built around this time contained royal insignias, fine textiles, and more than a ton of

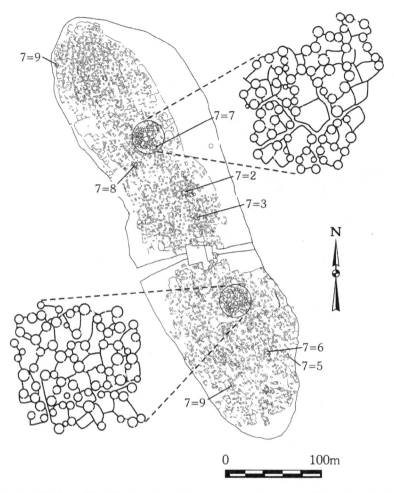

Figure 17 Plan of the Wanka site of Tunanmarca. Courtesy of Timothy Earle.

other precious objects made from marine shell, semiprecious stones, gold, and other metals (Shimada 1996). There might have been more metal in that coastal crypt than was circulating throughout Wanka territories during the century before the Inca conquest.

Archaeological assemblages from Wanka houses and burials indicate a society where significant surpluses were not produced, and there is no evidence for the specialized production and trade of fine craft goods (D'Altroy and Hastorf 2001). The economic strategies of Wanka households emphasized crop diversity, strong kin networks, and investments to reduce the risks posed by seasonal raiding and large-scale warfare. Wanka families did not labor to support priests, officials, or a nobility that lived lavishly on their tributes. Instead, colonial witnesses recalled that their ancestors "recognized as lords the bravest men . . . and to these they gave no tribute other than to show them respect and keep their fields for them. And these [war leaders] were valued based on what they acquired from the spoils of war" (Vega et al. 1965[c. 1580]:169). Based on household excavations, successful raids did not carry off much in the way of riches – llamas and food were the most likely plunder. Although the emphasis on male militarism cannot be denied, warfare was not incessant. It is noteworthy that women's shawl pins were among the few elite adornments worn by high-status Wankas (D'Altroy and Hastorf 2001), highlighting poorly understood roles that elite women performed in everyday life and community politics.

The general characteristics of Wanka settlements and social organization are typical of most of the central Andean highlands in the century before Inca conquest, and the political decentralization, economic underdevelopment, and heightened militarism across the region facilitated rapid Inca expansion. The first expedition to reach the Mantaro Valley sent messengers in advance of the vast imperial army, offering gifts and marriage alliances to war leaders who submitted without fighting. According to one early chronicler (Cieza de León 1880[c. 1553:chapter 49]), the Wankas rejected these inducements and sent 40,000 fighters against the invaders. After prevailing in a bloody battle, the Incas showed clemency, inspiring Wanka leaders to come to them to promise tribute and faithful service. The Incas appointed the first who submitted as *curacas*, and they ordered them to provide labor for farming and textile production, and to give young women for royal service (Vega et al. 1965[c. 1580]:169).

The Wankas' existing focus on rain-fed horticulture and herding presented clear opportunities for the expanding empire, which used labor tribute to cultivate productive lands and develop new roads, waystations, settlements, and storehouses in unoccupied valley-bottom areas. Unlike the Cuzco region, where royal estate construction created huge systems of canal-fed terraces, the floor of the Mantaro Valley was not appropriated and transformed in the same manner. The hilltop towns of Hatunmarca and Tunanmarca shrank as many Wanka families relocated closer to fertile valley-bottom fields, but the households that remained in the old towns still experienced effects of Inca rule (D'Altroy and Hastorf 2001). They used Inca-style pottery regularly and increased their consumption of maize and meat, changes that were especially marked in lower-status households. The overall impact of imperial rule was a flattening of the limited status distinctions that already existed, as well as a stronger tie to Inca-style goods that were produced within the province.

Changes occurring in the old hilltop towns were directly linked to the economic transformations taking place on the valley floor. The staple economy under Inca rule emphasized surplus production and state-administered storage, and the Incas had almost 3,000 single-room storehouses (*collca*) constructed at more than fifty complexes throughout the upper Mantaro Valley (D'Altroy and Hastorf 1984). Such facilities served a practical function while also communicating an abundance of goods that Inca representatives dispensed with generously as a performance of royal care and reciprocity. Maize was one of several crops that archaeologists encountered in storehouses near Hatun Xauxa, but quinoa, tubers, and *tarwi* (an Andean legume) were also present. Based on Wanka *quipu* records of goods taken by early Spanish expeditions, it appears that some storehouses also held pottery, blankets, and sandals for the use of soldiers and state travelers (Espinoza Soriano 1971). The capital of the Wanka province was Hatun Xauxa, a new administrative center built along the royal road from Cuzco to Quito. The site had a permanent population of several thousand households, and its large central plaza accommodated tens of thousands of Inca subjects who gathered periodically for administrative events and festivals. Spaniards who visited Hatun Xauxa during one such gathering in 1533 described how the streets surrounding the main plaza were packed with people exchanging goods they had brought with them (H. Pizarro 1968[1533]:129).

Excavations in Wanka households demonstrate some subtle, yet significant, developments to local economies under Inca rule (Costin and Earle 1989). Before Inca conquest, Wanka people acquired virtually all food locally, and they made most of their tools from local stone. Almost all pottery was consumed close to where it was produced. Wanka households sometimes made regional exchanges to acquire high-quality lithic material and metal, but their only long-distance trading was for marine shell, which was exceedingly rare before the Inca conquest. Under Inca imperial rule, households increased their consumption of everyday goods produced throughout the region, diversifying their diets and acquiring lithic material and pottery more frequently from neighboring communities. Inca-style pottery produced in the region was well distributed at the provincial capital, as well as among populations still living in hilltop communities. Significantly, the evidence from Wanka households does not indicate a major increase in the accumulation of wealth goods or participation in long-distance networks. Small amounts of marine shell still reached the region, and there was a slight increase in metal and pottery from more than 30 miles (50 km) away. Nevertheless, coca leaf, tin bronze, and Chimú blackware pottery were rare in Inca-era Wanka households, suggesting that the Inca state did not promote long-distance trade or encourage the accumulation of wealth among their Wanka subjects. The regional peace accompanying Inca rule promoted a sense of local abundance, but it did not stimulate market development.

Under Inca rule, some Wanka men gained power and performed important roles in mobilizing the provincial political economy. The highest-ranking *curacas* held administrative titles to reward their early support for Inca expansion, and those who remained loyal were able to pass them on to their sons and grandsons. The creation of newly made provincial lords among the Wankas contrasts with the Callejón de Huaylas, an extensive highland valley in northern Peru where royal marriages to local noblewomen promoted imperial interests. Two Huaylas women married the Inca Huayna Capac, and they administered approximately 12,000 tributary households as noble fiefs (Espinoza Soriano 1976). The personal connections between the Huaylas nobility and the Inca palace might explain the limited Inca footprint in the valley, where there is evidence of an Inca road but no major administrative center.

Although the remains of Inca roads, waystations, and storage facilities survive along the corridors connecting Cuzco to the northern frontiers, large administrative centers are rare throughout northern Peru. The Incas built a provincial center at Cajamarca – where the Spaniards captured Atahualpa in 1532 – that facilitated expansion into the Chachapoya region and neighboring lowlands. They also established an administrative center estimated at 25 hectares at Huamachuco (Topic and Topic 1993). Inca sites in other parts of northern Peru (e.g., Cajas, Huancabamba) are much smaller than those centers, and away from the Inca roads, archaeological surveys often encounter very little Inca-style pottery, suggesting limited impact on rural settlement and subsistence patterns.

The Huánuco Region

When Francisco Pizarro journeyed from Cajamarca to Cuzco in 1533, he traveled through the Callejón de Huaylas instead of taking the imperial road through the neighboring Callejón de Conchucos. In doing so, the *conquistadores* bypassed the largest highland Inca center, Huánuco Pampa, a 200-hectare city that was built in a remote location along the royal road (Figure 18). Like Hatun Xauxa, this site featured a huge central plaza that easily accommodated tens of thousands of people, as well as a complex of roughly 500 single-room structures where maize, potatoes, textiles, and other goods were kept for state purposes. Unlike the Wanka provincial center, Huánuco Pampa was a disembedded capital established far from the groups that served it, and the Huánuco region offers a well-documented contrast to the economic changes seen through the excavation of Wanka households under Inca rule.

Whereas the expansive upper Mantaro Valley sustained tens of thousands of people who identified as Wanka, the Huánuco region was home to numerous smaller groups, including the Chupaychus, Wamalies, and Yachas (Morris and

Figure 18 Plan of the Inca provincial capital at Huánuco Pampa.

Thompson 1985). They lived in narrow valleys feeding the upper Huallaga and Marañón Rivers, which traversed warm and humid landscapes on a steep descent from the snowcapped Andes to the Amazonian lowlands. Before Inca conquest, many local villages were situated on remote ridgetops and other places that afforded visibility and natural defenses, although there is little evidence that residents invested substantial labor in fortifications. Settlements like Wakan and Wamalli were much smaller than those of the Wanka, with most consisting of a few dozen houses scattered across the habitable parts of a ridge or flat place (Matos Mendieta, in Murra 1972) (Figure 19). The few archaeologically documented sites in the region show considerable architectural variation, reflecting cultural diversity before and during Inca rule. In 1549, Spanish officials visited more than 140 settlements subject to the Chupaychus, and their inventory of houses complements the limited archaeological evidence (Murra 1967). Across a region once settled by several thousand tributary households, there was just one village with more than 100 houses. Most settlements were hamlets with fewer than twenty houses, indicating a landscape where households and extended families managed everyday affairs and had only occasional contact with powerful imperial officials.

Although the local groups of the Huánuco region were highlanders, many lived at relatively low elevations on the Amazonian slope, where subsistence practices focused on a different array of crops and wild resources. The Chupaychus settled in a dispersed pattern across a landscape that was 1,500 m (approximately one vertical mile) lower than the hilltops where the Wankas

Figure 19 Domestic architecture at the site of Wakan, a local pre-Inca village in the Huánuco region. Photo courtesy of the Division of Anthropology, AMNH.

built their principal towns. Resources that the Wankas could only acquire through long-distance exchanges – coca leaf, tropical hardwoods, gold – were locally available to the Chupaychus and their neighbors, who farmed different strains of maize, as well as tubers, fruits, and other crops more suited to their local landscapes. The wild animals that could be hunted on Chupaychu lands were also different from those grazing on the high grasslands surrounding Wanka towns. For example, the Tingo María National Park, located just 100 km downstream from the modern city of Huánuco, is home to tapir, peccary, ocelot, and several species of monkey.

The Incas took advantage of these locally available lowland resources in their administration of the Huánuco region. The 1549 Spanish *visita* mentioned (Murra 1967) numerous small villages and hamlets occupied by labor colonists (*mitimaes*) that included ethnic Incas and members of resettled groups, such as the Yaros and Queros. Among the local and resettled populations, most households grew maize on Inca fields or produced other staples destined for Inca storehouses. There were also hamlets and households of *camayos* whose service to the Inca consisted of working tropical hardwoods into drinking cups (*queroscamayos*), cultivating coca leaves (*cocacamayos*), growing cotton, gathering honey, panning for gold, and working colorful feathers. In addition to wealth production, other *camayos* made salt, pottery, sandals, and cordage, or staffed the frontier forts and waystations along the Inca roads into the lowlands. Although we lack a sample of excavated households from the Huánuco region, the early documents describing rural wealth production offer a strong contrast with the Inca political economy in the Wanka provinces, where labor service and staple production were the central elements.

In the high grasslands to the west of the Chupaychu villages, the Incas made considerable investments in infrastructure along their Cuzco–Quito road. In addition to well-built roads and waystations, they constructed nearly 4,000 stone buildings at Huánuco Pampa, located several days' walk from the Chupaychus and other subject populations. Imperial officials laid out a series of great halls (often called *kallankas*) around an enormous central plaza, and they built an administrative palace, an *acllahuasi* cloister, and a sun temple nearby (Morris and Thompson 1985). As in other provincial settings, they constructed rows of storehouses on the nearby hillslopes above the site, although Hatun Xauxa, a much smaller site, had four times as many *collcas* at nearby storage complexes, and thousands more scattered throughout the upper Mantaro Valley. Huánuco Pampa was built at an urban scale, but extensive excavations indicate that only a few state-associated compounds were occupied year-round (Morris et al. 2011). While a few state officials – many of them women – resided there permanently, most local subjects spent little time there, probably on festive occasions that included administrative reviews and ritual performances where Inca officials reciprocated labor services with food and drink.

Excavations in several hundred structures at Huánuco Pampa have encountered few wealth goods, which is surprising for a provincial capital that administered so many subjects whose labor service focused on acquiring raw materials and creating fine craft products. There appear to be no workshops for the state-supervised manufacture of artisan goods, although concentrations of weaving tools in the *acllahuasi* complex and palace indicate textile production by religious women (Morris and Thompson 1985). In the administrative palace, there were few metal tools or adornments, most of which were bronze or copper, and the excavation assemblage of nearly 100,000 sherds included fewer than 2,000 fragments of Inca polychrome pottery (Morris et al. 2011). By comparison, UMARP archaeologists picked up 6,000 Inca polychrome fragments in surface collections at Hatun Xauxa and excavated another 20,000 from Wanka households (D'Altroy and Hastorf 2001). Imperial pottery is almost completely absent in Inca-era villages in the Huánuco region.

Although little wealth appeared in the excavations at Huánuco Pampa, colonial documents indicate that considerable amounts of exotic raw materials and finished craft goods arrived at the site, most of which were taken to Cuzco for Inca use. In 1549, Paucar Guaman, the paramount Chupaychu lord, described the goods produced by the 4,000 households under his command, identifying the ultimate destination for many products after they were delivered to imperial officials (Table 1; see Murra 1967).

His successor, don Diego Xagua, added critical details on the provincial economy in testimony that he gave in 1562 (Murra 1967). Inca subjects grew maize on Inca fields and carried the harvest to Huánuco Pampa, a seven-day journey. They also cultivated and transported coca leaf. Of the fine cloth taken to the provincial capital, Xagua said that half was sent on to Cuzco, along with the best of the featherwork, sandals, salt, and chili peppers. All silver and gold produced in the province was sent on to Cuzco – there were severe penalties for withholding it, and he explicitly stated that there were no silversmiths living in the province. By contrast, all ceramics produced in the province were used locally.

Xagua testified that the Inca "did not impose on them a *tasa* [annual levy] of what they had to give, other than setting aside lands for them to cultivate and naming the number of natives that had to mine gold and silver." As already noted, the earlier description of Chupaychu tribute gives an approximate count of households occupied in specific labors, indicating that Inca demands could

Table 1 Chupaychu tribute products and their destinations

Product	Households	To Huánuco	To Cuzco
Featherwork	20		
Honey	60		
Fine cloth	400		
Dyes and pigments	40		
Llamas/alpacas	240		
Maize		X	X
Chili peppers	40		X
Salt	40–60		
Coca	60	X	X
Sandals	40	X	X
Wood cups and bowls	40		X
Pottery	40	X	
Other agricultural products	500		

vary from year to year. For example, there might be forty, fifty, or sixty households engaged in salt-making at different times. Both Paucar Guaman and Xagua testified that hundreds of Chupaychu households were permanently resettled to the Cuzco region to labor as farmers, builders, and royal servants. In addition to their peacetime services, the Chupaychus periodically sent hundreds of soldiers for Inca campaigns.

The rural settlements of Huánuco produced staple surpluses and craft goods that funded provincial administration and provided for those traveling Inca roads on state business. They also produced valuable raw materials and wealth goods, which they delivered to Inca officials, who sent the finest on to Cuzco. Tributary populations reportedly did not consume those goods unless they received them as gifts from the Inca. They apparently did not participate in long-distance trade with other Inca subjects, although it is possible that they acquired some goods (e.g., feathers, honey) through barter with independent lowland groups. When asked, Xagua explicitly stated that there were no merchants (*mercaderes*) or full-time specialists (*oficios*) living among the Chupaychu (Murra 1967). Instead of merchant caravans plying their trade up and down the new imperial road network, imperial officials channeled select resources and people from Huánuco southward to Cuzco, supporting the production of wealth goods for palace consumption and state sacrifices. State travelers journeying northward from Cuzco included troops bound for the Quito frontier, as well as administrative and religious officials who stayed in the lodgings built by Inca subjects and fed and clothed themselves from the supplies kept in Inca *collcas*.

The Titicaca Basin

The Mantaro and Huánuco cases illustrate distinct ways that Inca provincial administration stimulated the large-scale cultivation and storage of maize to feed state laborers and support festive events. Maize intensification was less feasible as the Incas conquered to the southeast of Cuzco, where most groups lived in places where the crop would not thrive. Although some maize farming is possible along the shores of Lake Titicaca (over 3,800 m asl), the high grasslands (*puna*) of the Collasuyu province were economically unfamiliar terrain for the Incas, a world that more readily generated surpluses of dried potatoes (*chuño*), dehydrated camelid meat (*charqui*) and wool, and fish from the lake. This region was also linguistically distinct from the predominantly Quechua-speaking groups living in the central highlands. The camelid pastoralists living in the region were mostly Aymara speakers, while the fisherfolk living on Lake Titicaca spoke Uru.

Inca witnesses described Aymara herding confederacies as powerful and wealthy kingdoms that rivaled their first emperors. The archaeological evidence contradicts this claim, instead indicating the same decentralized settlement patterns seen elsewhere in the central highlands. During the century or so before Inca conquest, populations moved to hilltop sites (*pucaras*), where new communities constructed impressive fortifications to protect themselves from intensifying warfare (Arkush 2010) (Figure 20). Some of these *pucara* sites grew to 25 hectares or more and contained hundreds of houses within their ringed defenses, but even the largest lacked public architecture, temples, and palatial residences. Although comparable in size to Wanka towns, the largest pre-Inca settlements in the Titicaca Basin were less densely settled, housing populations estimated in the low thousands.

Inca accounts of the conquest of the Titicaca Basin suggest that it was a drawn-out process that unfolded over generations as the expanding state established alliances with local leaders, carried out military expeditions, and returned to quash widespread rebellions (Stanish 2003). Reconquest provided Inca rulers with a justification for implementing more intensive administrative practices in the region, which included large-scale resettlement of populations from the high *pucara* sites to undefended towns and villages built along new imperial roads that ran near the lakeshore. As in the upper Mantaro Valley, the abandonment of hilltop sites might have been gradual, although the near absence of Inca-style pottery at Titicaca Basin *pucara* sites suggests that any

Figure 20 Aerial view of Pucarani, a *pucara* site from the Lake Titicaca Basin. Photo courtesy of Elizabeth Arkush.

remaining population did not acquire and use this imperial craft good to the extent that Wanka households did. At some *pucara* sites, Inca-style masonry can be seen in association with small religious shrines and burial structures, suggesting that those places remained important to local populations even as they settled into new communities.

The largest sites along the Inca roads in the Titicaca Basin were new towns, such as Hatunqolla and Chucuito, which were governed by Aymara lords who served the Inca (Hyslop 1984, 1990). There was no provincial capital like Huánuco Pampa where multiple ethnic groups could gather under the supervision of imperial officials, and no large storage complexes have been identified archaeologically. The largest Inca town in the region appears to be at Tiwanaku, where local populations associated the ruins of a pre-Inca state capital with universal creation myths (Yaeger and López Bejarano 2018). Aymara lords living in roadside towns often provided the kind of state-supported hospitality that was offered at imperial waystations (*tambo*) along other stretches of the royal road. High-ranking Lupaca administrators received llamas, maize, and coca leaf from Inca officials so that they could entertain state travelers and provision passing troops. Those lords described a close collaborative relationship between their ancestors and the Inca ruler (Diez de San Miguel 1964

[1567]), and their Inca-era population counts indicate a distinct settlement pattern from the provinces already discussed. The smallest Lupaca towns comprised nearly 1,500 tributary households, and the largest were more than twice as large. The Aymara and Uru populations living there were divided into moieties (*Anansaya* and *Lurinsaya*, similar to Cuzco's *hanan* and *hurin* divisions) administered by Aymara officials, who coordinated with smaller populations of *mitimaes* that lived nearby. Lupaca lords controlled large camelid herds and maintained maize-farming colonies in coastal valleys, including the Sama Valley, located roughly 200 km away in the northern reaches of the Atacama Desert.

Like the Chupaychus, Lupaca lords described their Inca-era tribute not as fixed annual payments (*tasas*) but as personal requests from their sovereign, which they would have been foolish to refuse. The Inca sometimes asked for soldiers, and they sent thousands of troops for his wars, many of whom never returned. At other times, the Inca requested laborers for construction projects in Cuzco, and they sent them there to work alongside royal *yanacona* and *mitimaes* from other provinces. The Lupacas kept camelid herds for the Inca in their own lands, and they cultivated fields along the lakeside, where they grew bitter potatoes and quinoa. Unmarried young men and women served the Inca by fishing, hunting game, trapping birds, and gathering land snails and mushrooms. Lupaca runners carried fresh fish to Cuzco, and on festive occasions, they drove llamas and alpacas there to be sacrificed. Ranging more broadly, the Lupacas cultivated maize fields for the Inca in the Cochabamba Valley (see Section 6), and they sent households to Inca mines to produce gold, silver, lead, and cinnabar. Some of this distant service was carried out by households designated as *mitimaes*, who were also resettled at frontier garrisons and highland centers like Hatun Xauxa (Diez de San Miguel 1964[1567]).

The local administration of Lupaca towns contrasts with the nearby Copacabana Peninsula, where the Incas established a restricted precinct where they resettled a large multiethnic population from dozens of nonlocal groups. This imperial enclave was under the direct administration of a noble Inca lord from Cuzco, and it served as the point of embarkation for travelers visiting Inca temples and shrines on the Islands of the Sun and Moon, where highland people celebrated the creation of the universe (Bauer and Stanish 2001) (Figure 21). The maintenance of hundreds of priestesses and other imperial officials required considerable resources, as did Inca-sponsored festivities and sacrifices. Maize beer and coca were consumed in large quantities, and recent underwater archaeology has recovered Inca offerings of gold, marine shell, and decorated pottery from the icy waters of Lake Titicaca (Delaere and

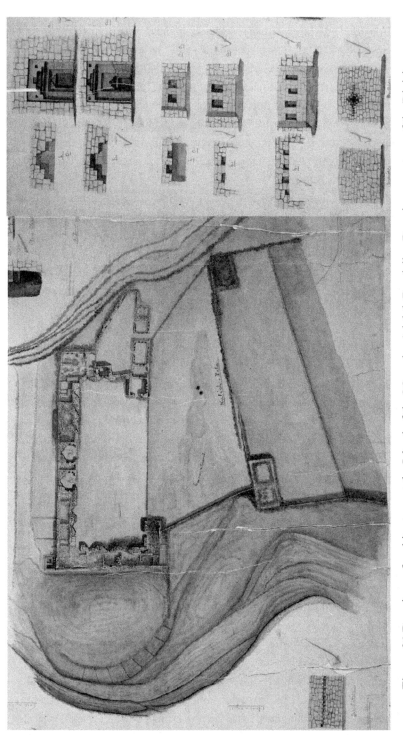

Figure 21 Drawings of architecture at the Island of the Moon by Adolph Bandelier. Drawings courtesy of the Division of Anthropology, AMNH.

Capriles 2020). All of these reflect imperial long-distance networks that used *camayos* to procure or transform rare and valuable things that were not locally available.

Trajectories of Economic Development

The three highland regions discussed here illustrate variations tied to local ecology and pre-Inca social organization. Although the empire invested strategically in infrastructure and demanded mining labor and local agropastoral production, many Inca services fluctuated from year to year, a feature of the political economy that is sometimes overlooked in discussions of Inca administration (cf. Julien 1988). Native witnesses observed that population sizes changed under Inca rule, growing in good times, but also declining when people died on imperial campaigns. One elderly Lupaca lord recalled that his people sent 5,000 soldiers to fight on the northern frontier, of whom only 1,000 returned (Diez de San Miguel 1964[1567]). The Incas facilitated tribute mobilization by setting aside resources (lands, herds, mines) to be worked for the ruler and the state religion, providing necessary tools and subsistence for nonlocal projects, and designating large numbers of resettled workers (*mitimaes*) and households with specialized tribute labor (*camayos*) for ongoing production tasks.

Regional variations in Inca political economy suggest some general developments that occurred during the century or so of imperial rule. Accounts of early imperial campaigns emphasize expenditures of staple and wealth goods from the Cuzco region, which fed troops, funded road construction, and provided royal gifts for local allies. Those who acknowledged Inca sovereignty mobilized labor tribute for imperial projects in and around their lands, while those who resisted were conquered and replaced with cooperative *curacas*. In both scenarios, the power of local leaders shifted, from organizing fortification construction and local raiding, to delivering labor for state projects that included military service, agricultural intensification, and the construction of state roads, waystations, and storehouses. Over time, imperial administration intensified through the development of new administrative facilities and governing hierarchies. Many chroniclers identify the tenth Inca, Topa Inca Yupanqui, as the ruler who built sites like Huánuco Pampa and appointed the *curaca* officials in the decimal hierarchy.

Witnesses from *mitima* communities often named his son, Huayna Capac, as the Inca who resettled them in small communities and charged them with specific ongoing labor assignments as *camayos*. The proliferation of resettlement and wealth-related service assignments suggests state attempts to promote labor specialization as a strategy for controlling subject populations and increasing sovereign wealth. The civil war that followed Huayna Capac's sudden death disrupted labor tribute across provincial regions, and it affected the highland networks connecting Cuzco and Quito (where most fighting took place) in profound ways. Provincial groups living near the royal roads saw thousands of their households conscripted and killed, and the rival armies consumed massive amounts of stockpiled goods in imperial storehouses, which had been used in peaceful times to feed state workers and fund ceremonies and festivities. When Pizarro and his men reached the highlands in 1532, many Inca centers were under military occupation, and institutions like the *acllahuasi*, which undergirded imperial religious life, were repurposed to weave and brew for Atahualpa's soldiers.

Conclusions

Trajectories of economic plasticity varied in the inner highland provinces, but there are some shared features across regions. As Inca rule redirected labor and built new infrastructure, the empire did not promote long-distance exchanges or the independent acquisition and display of personal wealth among subject populations. Instead of more wealth, groups like the Wanka increased their consumption of Inca-affiliated craft goods (decorated pottery, bronze). Ordinary people ate more meat and consumed more maize, some of it probably provided by the state. The staple finance practices that funded regional administration amassed stores of food and supplies to provide the hospitality that local people expected when working for others, and to stage celebratory feasts and ceremonies that reciprocated Inca relationships with subjects. Inca wealth production differed from the farming and herding practices that generated staple surpluses, but it also constituted a form of reciprocity. Whereas feeding state work crews and sponsoring imperial feasts fulfilled the social expectations that ordinary people had for their distant lord, the disposal of wealth as gifts and sacrifices emphasized the personal relationships that Inca royalty and religious officials maintained with powerful people and supernatural beings.

The ethos of reciprocity did more than bind subject and sovereign. Massive resources were mobilized for Inca ritual offerings intended to maintain universal order. Maize beer, coca leaf, marine shell, precious metal, fine cloth, camelids, and even children were given in mass quantities under different circumstances, representing the surpluses of entire provinces. These were hardly the only valuables disposed of outside of a strictly political-economic context. Staple goods from Inca storehouses supported troops traveling to the frontiers to subjugate people who rejected the supposed reciprocity that Inca subjects experienced. For a society that saw human subjects as a form of sovereign wealth, the costly wars to extend and hold empire's edge expended valuable sources of labor, offsetting provincial population growth and necessitating state interventions in household organization and marriage practices.

5 Specialization and Trade on the Pacific Coast

Inca gold and silver did not circulate widely in the inner highland provinces. Much of what was not displayed in Cuzco by the Inca nobility was buried in offerings, attached to the fine masonry of temples, and guarded in royal palaces and ancestral crypts. This is significant because Pizarro and his *conquistadores* arrived in the Andes seeking treasures they had acquired in Panama and Colombia, where local chiefs had long used elaborate gold adornments, gemstones, and other status markers. After a disastrous start to his explorations along the Pacific coast of Colombia and Ecuador, Pizarro began to encounter gold and other treasure as his ships approached the coastal margins of the Inca world, where local economies developed along a very different trajectory than those of the Andean highlands (Figure 22).

Ironically, the earliest written description of the sophisticated economies of Inca coastal valleys came in the form of an inventory of metal and textiles plundered in an act of Spanish piracy. In 1526, Pizarro's navigator, Bartolomé Ruiz, was scouting coastal waters when his ship captured a 30-ton balsa raft that was sailing north from Inca-governed lands. The vessel was on its outbound journey to warmer waters to trade for colorful *Spondylus* shell, and its cargo yielded a haul of gold jewelry – crowns, belts, bracelets, armbands, tweezers, and bells – as well as silver accessories (cups, mirrors, serving vessels), beads made of rock crystal and emeralds, and well-made blackware pottery. The ship also held stores of vibrantly dyed cloth and garments, which were intricately woven with patterns of birds, fish, animals, and trees (Relación Sámano-Xérez 1968[1527]). The people aboard carried balances to measure gold, silver, and other materials when they traded for marine shells and strands of colorful red and white beads made from them (Figure 23).

The Coastal *Yungas*

The riches that the Spaniards took from the captured trading ship resembled the lavish goods buried with Moche, Sicán, and Chimú elites, who ruled over the north coast of Peru for a millennium before the Incas conquered the region. The sheer amount of wealth taken from a single vessel reflects coastal

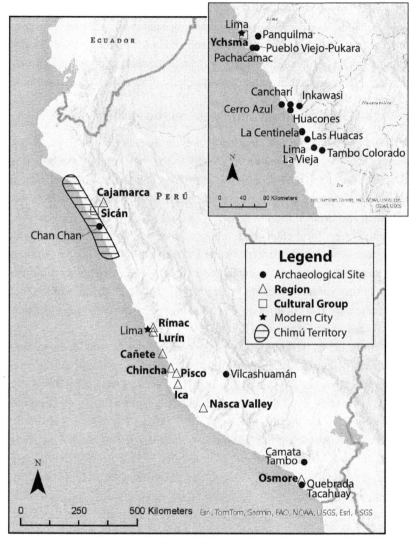

Figure 22 Map of the Pacific coast of the Inca Empire.

economies that generated vast staple surpluses, which supported artisans who produced status goods that were used to some extent in interregional trading. In the centuries before Inca expansion, coastal societies were more politically centralized, economically specialized, and socially stratified than highland groups. The distribution and socioeconomic functions of wealth goods on the Pacific coast differed sharply from conditions in the highlands, where late prehispanic leaders lacked access to the same opulent and abundant goods.

Figure 23 A strand of *Spondylus* shell beads (AMNH 41.2/8819) that might have been *chaquira*, which was used as a medium of exchange in Ecuador. Photo courtesy of the Division of Anthropology, AMNH.

This is in part because of the productivity of farming and fishing economies on the north coast, which continued to sustain urban populations, specialized artisans, and ruling dynasties after AD 1000, when fluctuating highland climates and social unrest contributed to widespread conditions of decentralization and the adoption of diversity-oriented subsistence practices. The valleys of the Pacific coast normally receive less precipitation than the Andean highlands or Amazonian lowlands, with increasing aridity as one moves southward from the mangrove swamps of Ecuador to the hyperarid Atacama Desert of Chile. To the Incas, the Pacific coast looked barren and dead, except for the river valleys where highland rain and glacial meltwater from the snowcapped Andean peaks sustained life (Figure 24). For thousands of years, coastal populations expanded these river oases by channeling out irrigation water to sustain agricultural fields in the floodplains. By the time of the Inca conquest, centuries of local canal construction had already developed most arable land, although the size and productivity of coastal field systems varied considerably. Today, the coastal rivers of northern Peru supply abundant water year-round to broad and fertile alluvial plains, whereas the narrow rivers at the edge of the south coast often become subterranean before reaching the Pacific, or only flow when recharged

Figure 24 Along the Peruvian coast, fertile river valleys cut into the dry coastal
desert. Photo from the site of Ungará in the Cañete Valley.

during the highland rainy season (December to March). Where irrigation water
was available, coastal farmers cultivated a wide range of crops, including maize,
ají peppers, beans, squash, and fruits, such as *lucuma* and *pacay* (Marcus 2016).
In many regions, farmers added guano (bird excrement) to their fields to
maintain soil fertility. Coastal valleys did not experience the freezing temperatures found in the highlands, and irrigation water and fertilizer use made it
possible to cultivate farmland year-round.

In addition to food, coastal agrarian landscapes also produced industrial
plants such as cotton, bulrush, gourds, wood (such as *huarango*), and cane,
some of which were vital for fishing populations. Coastal people used cotton to
make cloth and fishing nets, and they collected bulrush and other reeds to
construct their fishing boats. They fashioned gourds into containers and net
floats and used cane for building houses and other structures. Fishing communities exploited the abundant resources found in the cold waters of the Pacific.
For more than 10,000 years, human populations had fished in the ocean,
collected shellfish in the shallows, and hunted sea birds and marine mammals
living along the shore (Prieto and Sandweiss 2020). The ocean provided
bountiful resources and allowed fishing groups to practice a more sedentary
lifestyle early on, and the addition of irrigation agriculture led to urban occupations. Although most marine resources replenished themselves when used
sustainably, their availability fluctuated significantly every few years due to

cyclical climatic shifts associated with the El Ñino Southern Oscillation (ENSO) phenomenon. Changes in the currents and temperature of offshore waters meant that the types of animals and resources available sometimes varied from year to year. Strong ENSO events could also bring unwelcome rainfall to the coast, creating mudslides that devastated agricultural lands and settlements. These ecological and climatic factors combined to create an abundant, but sometimes unpredictable, environment.

Political Continuity and Change

The Incas designated the present-day Peruvian coastline as part of their Chinchaysuyu and Contisuyu provinces. The Chinchaysuyu coast included the territories of the Chimú Empire (north coast) and the valleys whose religious practices were shaped by pilgrimages to the creation shrine of Pachacamac (central and south coast). In these areas, local societies were more hierarchical and economically specialized than the early Inca societies of the Cuzco region. Farther to the south, in Contisuyu, coastal valleys at the edge of the Atacama Desert were much narrower, lacking the reliable river flows and extensive floodplains that supported large urban populations in the north. Regardless of these differences among coastal regions, the integration of a variety of special-ized laborers – from farmers and fisherfolk to artisans and merchants – was central to Inca political economy on the coast. Artisans trained in coastal workshops possessed desired skillsets, technologies, and raw materials that could enhance Inca wealth production, and the agricultural bounty of irrigated coastal farmlands could be stored and redistributed by state officials in places where they could commandeer or construct access to water and land.

Some of the coastal societies of Chinchaysuyu already had bureaucratic practices related to the processing and storage of information. On the central and south coast, knotted-cord records collected in the Nasca and Rímac valleys show the use of a base-five system to store numerical information during the Middle Horizon period (c. AD 600–1000), long before the proliferation of the Inca *quipu* (Figure 25) (Conklin 1982; Shady et al. 2000). Although the continuity of such practices is unclear after AD 1000, quipu use was widespread along the central and south coast under Inca rule. By contrast, Inca quipus are rare on the north coast, where the Chimú Empire is thought to have used repetitive architectural forms to accomplish similar functions. Chimú palace enclosures (called *ciudadelas*) contain large numbers of identical niched U-shaped structures that John Topic (2003) proposes were used for bureaucratic meetings and to process and store information about different types of goods kept in the enclosures. Although more work needs to be done to clarify the

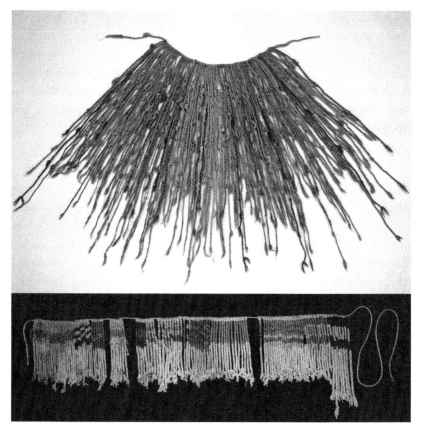

Figure 25 The Incas used *quipus* (top, Courtesy of the AMNH Library, Asset ID: ptc-3614, B/8705) throughout the empire to record information about labor, the decimal system of administration, and tribute goods. While expanded by the Incas, the use of textile record-keeping devices has pre-Inca roots, as evidenced by Middle Horizon examples (bottom, Courtesy of the Division of Anthropology, AMNH 41.2/7678).

chronology of different information management practices, some coastal societies were clearly accustomed to processing and storing information before they became Inca subjects.

To the extent possible, the Incas restructured, coopted, and amplified preexisting political and economic practices based on their administrative goals and their relationships with local elites. In areas with dense occupation and a high degree of economic specialization, imperial officials often had to focus on social and religious methods of integration to expand their empire and incorporate existing networks into their political economy. This included transforming burial rituals (Dalton et al. 2022) and integrating coastal religious practices, such as pilgrimages to the oracle of Pachacamac and veneration of the ocean. While aligning their sun cult with coastal beliefs and practices, the Incas also attempted to establish their decimal system of administration in many coastal areas, which was central to their ability to transmit administrative demands and store economic information. To reorganize the coastal wealth economy, they reportedly resettled skilled workers to Cuzco (Rowe 1948) and the south and central coasts (Rostworowski 1999).

The Inca approach to staple economies on the coast was less heavy-handed, limited to new irrigation canals and terraces in the few areas not already developed by coastal societies, such as foothill (*chaupi yunga*) landscapes that lay above the canal outtakes for floodplain irrigation networks (Dillehay 1977; Rostworowski 1988). The narrow foothill valleys could be irrigated and terraced to produce coca and other low-elevation crops, and Inca sites built there anchored new routes that bound the coastal provinces to imperial networks in the highlands. The Incas also developed a coastal road network that connected local centers and the new temples and administrative palaces that they built nearby. Although comparable to highland constructions in many ways, this new infrastructure was established alongside and within existing local networks, linking the empire to complex coastal economies that differed in important ways in their staple economies and wealth strategies.

Additional research on coastal political economies is still needed. Early Inca witnesses often ignored or described their populations in only general terms, as *yungas*, a term they also used to refer to the Amazonian lowlands lying to the east of the Andes. The highlands-centered narratives of early colonial chronicles strongly shaped modern anthropological interpretations of the Inca Empire, even though scholars such as Murra (2017[1969]) recognized the distinct social and economic organization of the coast. During the late twentieth century, Andean ethnographers focused primarily on highland communities whose size and ecological practices differed significantly from prehistoric coastal polities. The proliferation of archaeological research on the coast holds out great promise for filling in evidentiary gaps and developing new economic interpretations, although continuities in local artifacts and architecture often make it difficult to differentiate between pre-Inca and Inca-era occupations without absolute dating techniques. Much of the surface-level architecture in coastal valleys reflects Inca-era organization and activities, and excavations are needed to fully reconstruct pre-Inca site layouts and practices. A clearer understanding of pre-Inca political economies on the coast brings into focus how the Inca political economy transformed and incorporated local institutions.

Chinchaysuyu Coast

Scholars originally reconstructed processes of Inca coastal expansion using the colonial chronicles. The first expedition reportedly began during the reign of Pachacuti Inca Yupanqui, whose half-brother Capac Yupanqui led an army into Chimú lands after defeating the highland lord of Cajamarca, who was a close Chimú ally (Rowe 1948:42–43). Having received reinforcements from Cuzco, Capac Yupanqui invaded and conquered Chimú territory, sacking the capital, Chan Chan, and carrying treasure and skilled metal-workers back to Cuzco. Inca forces capitalized on the victory by conducting additional campaigns to the north and south of Chimú territory. Recent dates from the central and south coast challenge this narrative and indicate an Inca presence in some areas by around 1400, approximately seventy years prior to the conventional timeline (Dalton 2020; Valdez and Bettcher 2022). Additional dates are needed from the north coast to clarify the chronology of Inca expansion into Chimú territories.

During the centuries prior to Inca conquest, the political organization of coastal valleys south of Tumbes (Peru) to the Acarí River differed sharply from the shifting settlement patterns and political decentralization seen in the central Andean highlands at that time (see Sections 3 and 4). Many coastal valleys had urban centers and centralized governing hierarchies that oversaw trade and warfare with neighboring groups (Castro and Ortega Morejón 1938[1553]). Economically specialized groups occupied each valley. Inland agriculturalists and coastal fisherfolk were the most common, but there were also several types of occupational specialists, from brewers to silversmiths and weavers. People participated in inter-group transactions at various scales; this included exchanges among specialized fishing and farming groups to meet subsistence needs and acquire raw material to make tools, as well as long-distance trade with other valleys and regions, some of it carried out by merchants (Hirth and Pillsbury 2013; Topic 2013).

Despite early colonial references to pre-Inca trade along the coast, there has been limited archaeological research to reconstruct intervalley exchange practices during this period, aside from the identification of long-distance trade goods, such as metals and *Spondylus* shell. Because the methods for understanding coastal economies remain underdeveloped, additional research is needed to determine the extent and volume of exchange at multiple scales, a necessary baseline for understanding how the Incas inserted themselves into, and altered, existing networks.

Incorporation of the Chimú Empire

Along the north coast of Peru, the Incas faced their most formidable opponent, the Chimú Empire, which controlled the lower valleys across a stretch of more than 500 km. The Chimú capital, Chan Chan, was the largest city in South America, housing tens of thousands of people, including the descendants of the ruling dynasty. The Chimú nobility lived in massive walled palaces called *ciudadelas*, which dominated the city center (Figure 26). Surrounding the *ciudadelas* were religious complexes, mid-level elite compounds, and dense warrens of small and irregularly laid out low-status households. Some of the lower-status neighborhoods housed artisans who produced fine craft goods for the Chimú elite. When their forces took Chan Chan, Inca rulers gained access to the city's immense wealth and highly specialized labor force, which contributed to new displays of royal splendor in Cuzco.

Although some farmers lived in the poorer parts of Chan Chan, most resided outside of the city, where the level of integration across different valley groups fluctuated through time. In some places farming and fishing populations might have been ethnically distinct (Netherly 1984; Prieto and Sandweiss 2020). The borders and divisions between groups were often tied to canals and access to

Figure 26 Ciudadelas at the site of Chan Chan, from the Shippee-Johnson Collection (Courtesy of the AMNH Library, Asset ID: 334890).

arable land, as canals and water management were essential for sustaining life in these regions and required cooperative use and regular upkeep. Along the north coast, the Chimú Empire incorporated local polities, governing them through a bureaucratic system that focused on economic exploitation rather than common religious practices (Mackey 2010; Vogel 2018). As their empire expanded, the Chimú built new infrastructure at strategic valley locations to control canals, and constructed administrative compounds to house officials who were sent to the provinces to exact tribute and administer local groups. Although group labor projects and redistribution were important, tribute was also critical for financing the state and elite households.

The Chimú and preceding polities, such as the Sicán and Lambayeque, had well-established populations of craft specialists, who produced fine ceramics, textiles, metal artifacts, and featherwork that were regularly deposited in elite tombs. The abundance of mortuary offerings indicates that local societies were highly stratified and hierarchical, and that many individuals could accumulate material wealth. The Chimú controlled exchange to Ecuador for *Spondylus* and precious gems and metals (Pillsbury 1996) and traded with communities in the *chaupi yunga* and nearby highlands (Topic 2013:340). In exchanges in northern Peru and Ecuador, axe- and I-shaped metal tokens served as potential mediums of exchange and status items that facilitated the growing wealth economy (Shimada and Merkel 2021).

Under Inca rule, dramatic demographic shifts took place in the Chimú heartland. Inca witnesses said that the Chimú ruler was carried off into exile in Cuzco, along with families of metalworkers who now produced adornments and other goods for Inca royalty. While curtailing the political power of the Chimú nobility, the Incas also reportedly dismantled Chimú control of long-distance trade with Ecuadorian groups, transferring power to polities from the south and central coasts, such as the Chincha (Carter 2011; Sandweiss and Reid 2016). Chan Chan appears to have lost much of its population, and there are references to Chimú people being resettled as *mitimaes* (Rostworowski 1999; Rowe 1948). There is relatively little Inca-related pottery present at the former Chimú capital, and there is evidence that some parts of the city were repurposed as burial mounds. The royal *ciudadelas* were largely abandoned, although other parts of the site might have continued to be occupied. The once densely populated Moche Valley experienced a population decline.

Beyond the capital area, Inca rule did not transform local practices substantially. To restructure Chimú political power, the Incas built new highland centers at Huamuchuco and Cajamarca, which presumably helped to administer coastal valleys where the empire promoted several lower-order Chimú centers, such as Farfán, to serve its interests locally (Mackey 2010; Mackey and Sapp 2021).

Figure 27 Inca road in northern Peru from the Hyslop archive, courtesy of the Division of Anthropology, AMNH.

Inca coastal networks built on preexisting infrastructure, such as roads (Figure 27) and strategically located sites, which were developed to meet the empire's needs. New workshops, storage features, and administrative complexes were established at some sites, whose oversight was entrusted to local lords. Few *quipus* have been recovered from the former Chimú territory, although some sites contain features apparently used for counting, such as *yupanas* (Barraza et al. 2022), which imperial officials presumably used to process and quantify information about tribute goods and labor groups. Chimú-Inca elites who governed at Inca-affiliated sites were still buried with textiles, fine ceramics, *Spondylus* shell, and metal items (Mackey and Nelson 2020), even if their access to long-distance trade goods diminished somewhat from earlier times. Compared with local highland lords, Inca subalterns on the north coast still invested considerable resources to display their wealth in life and death. Coastal elites used wealth goods to express social and ethnic identities, as well as their Inca connections, and it is not surprising that new aesthetics emerged. Local workshops added Inca and hybrid wares to their existing repertoires (Hayashida 1999), and new workshops at Chimú-Inca centers such as Farfán indicate stylistic mixing by local elites (Mackey 2010).

Inca Expansion and the Pachacamac Ritual Network

To the south of the former Chimú Empire, the Incas engaged with hierarchical societies on the central coast that had not been unified under a single government. Colonial records describe a political environment where alliances and boundaries were constantly shifting, which had effects on claims to irrigation water, land, and exchange relationships (Rostworowski 1977). Land was inherited within each coastal polity, and to meet Inca demands, elites allowed people to farm their lands (Castro and Ortega Morejón 1938[1553]). Regionally, groups cooperated and competed with each other. These negotiations included populations living in neighboring coastal valleys, in the coastal foothills (*chaupi yunga*), and in nearby highland areas.

One important pre-Inca polity was the Ychsma, who united different ethnic groups living in the Rímac and Lurín Valleys, the location of modern Lima. The focal point of their ritual economy was the site of Pachacamac, a shrine where coastal peoples converged in Inca times to give reverence to the creator of the Andean world. Pachacamac was already a sacred destination in pre-Inca times, where many groups brought their dead for burial. The style of burials at Pachacamac varies widely, some with sparse goods and others containing fine textiles, metal artifacts, ceramics, and balances, some of which were presumably used during economic transactions.

The Incas promoted the cult of Pachacamac, using it to build imperial power and elite alliances along the central and south coast (Makowski 2014). Beyond its importance as a ritual center, Pachacamac became an important junction where the Inca coastal road connected to the branch route that led to the highland center of Hatun Xauxa. Under Inca rule, many groups associated with the Pachacamac shrine network enjoyed increased access to long-distance coastal trade goods, particularly highly polished blackware vessels from the north coast and *Spondylus* shell from the warm waters of Ecuador. Their growing wealth consumption contrasts with former Chimú territories, where *Spondylus* use decreased as Inca control shifted maritime trade toward groups from the central and south coast (Carter 2011; Sandweiss and Reid 2016). The increased access to coastal trade goods was associated with the developing political and economic roles of Inca officials. Growing trade networks and wealth consumption appear to have been restricted to coastal areas. The Wankas, who lived just 150 km to the northeast of Pachacamac, did not experience this same increase in prestige goods.

The importance of Pachacamac for building Inca power on the central and south coast demonstrates the close relationship between Inca religious ideology and the imperial economy (Figure 28). As they did at the highland creation shrines in the Lake Titicaca Basin (see Section 4), the Incas incorporated aspects of local coastal religious ideology to bolster their imperial legitimacy. They used Pachacamac and other religious sites to build relationships, exert control, and collect tribute. The *conquistador* Hernando Pizarro reported that tributes

Figure 28 Photograph of architecture at the site of Pachacamac (Courtesy of the AMNH Library, Asset ID: K10632).

were offered to religious officials at Pachacamac, rather than being sent on to Cuzco. Goods collected and stored there were thus part of the ritual economy, which helped the Incas build their authority (Eeckhout 2012). The Incas heavily modified the organization and function of the site, building a Sun temple in a previously occupied location, as well as a restricted residential complex for the *mamacona* priestesses who staffed it. For administrative interactions, they built the Tauri Chumpi palace, which served as both an important Inca *tambo* and a center for local administration (Eeckhout and López-Hurtado 2018).

Before Inca projects altered Pachacamac, storage was located within restricted elite compounds. The Incas increased the storage capacity of the site and concentrated it around public spaces, similar to imperial facilities found in other parts of the empire. At Pachacamac, however, these public spaces were associated with ritual sectors, demonstrating the importance of state investments in the ritual economy (Eeckhout 2012). Imperial craft production at Pachacamac and on the central coast built on local production centers and networks (Chacaltana et al. 2023; Davenport 2020). Information about the type and quantity of goods stored at Pachacamac was probably encoded in the multiple *quipus* that have been recovered from the site. The *quipus* from Pachacamac show considerable structural diversity, possibly because the tribute and goods stored at Pachacamac came from diverse groups participating in the regional pilgrimage network.

Beyond the Pachacamac religious precinct, Inca administration in the Lurín and Rímac valleys took many forms and was based on environmental factors and political negotiations with a variety of leaders. Some sites, such as Panquilma, saw their power decline under Inca rule, while other groups had their authority elevated (Eeckhout and López-Hurtado 2018). The strategic manipulation of coastal religious sites and political elites contrasts with the more intensive Inca occupation of the Andean foothills. There is a marked Inca presence at the *chaupi yunga* site of Pueblo Viejo-Pukara, where the Incas built storage facilities and resettled highland populations. The site was important for local security and for supervising agricultural production and overseeing herds (Makowski 2002).

In the Cañete Valley to the south of Pachacamac, the Incas built Inkawasi, an administrative center, in a similar foothill location (Figure 29). This was a massive Inca installation that included at least 202 storehouses and residences, and it served as a regional center for tribute collection and administration (Snead 1992). Excavations by the Peruvian archaeologist Alejandro Chu have encountered *quipus* in association with stored staple goods, providing valuable perspectives on record-keeping practices at imperial centers (Urton and Chu 2015).

Figure 29 The site of Inkawasi in the Cañete Valley was a large Inca administrative center constructed along an Inca road. Excavations at the site recovered storage deposits and a large collection of *quipus*.

As the Incas invested in the *chaupi yunga* zone of the Cañete Valley, prolonged resistance by the Huarco polity required an extensive military campaign in the lower valley. Following the Inca victory, Inca architectural elements and material culture were integrated into lower-valley sites such as Canchari, Huacones (Vilca-huasi), and Cerro Azul, but large Inca administrative and storage features are conspicuously absent. At Cerro Azul, the Incas marked the local sacred landscape with an impressive masonry wall along a cliffside overlooking the sea (Marcus et al. 1985). The wall, which resembles stonework in the Cuzco region, was accompanied by three ritual structures built in a location that was highly visible from the water, a marked departure from the pre-Inca ritual structures built at the shrine. Outside of its Inca-associated ritual area, Cerro Azul functioned as an important economic center, a location for intensive fish processing where massive hauls of anchovies and sardines were dried. As with many coastal sites that were prominent at the time of Inca incorporation, it is not clear which surface-level architecture at Cerro Azul reflects pre-Inca and Inca-era investments, but the site became an important symbol of Inca power.

On the central coast, the Incas intensively occupied parts of the *chaupi yunga*, while their interactions with groups nearer to the coast were more indirect, focused on ideological control and interactions with local elites. Imperial administration used the powerful oracle of Pachacamac as a means of collecting tribute and gaining access to marine resources, lowland agricultural products, and long-distance trade goods. Administrative centers also were focused along the coastal road, and routes connecting to highland centers, such as Hatun Xauxa.

South Coast

Dates from archaeological excavations and local historical sources, particularly the *Relación de Chincha* (Castro and Ortega Morejón 1938[1558]), point to the incorporation of Peru's south coast under Pachacuti around 1400. That account describes multiple stages of Inca expansion into the Chincha Valley, beginning when the general Capac Yupanqui arrived and gave gifts to the Chincha elites, claiming to be the son of the Sun and asking for labor and land. After this initial encounter, the Incas steadily increased their demands, building storehouses, and formalizing road networks that connected Chincha to Pachacamac and Cuzco (Rostworowski 1999). The Inca ruler reportedly assigned priestesses (*mamacona*) to serve in the valley, with lands designated for their support; and he might have reordered the existing hierarchy of local nobles to resemble decimal units, while leaving the Chincha ruler in power.

The Inca incorporation of the south-coast valleys closest to Pachacamac – Chincha, Pisco, Ica, and Nasca – was similar in many ways to the interactions described for the central coast. This is not surprising, given that many south-coast elites probably participated in political and religious gatherings at Pachacamac, and their economies and material culture were similar. The Chincha relied on a specialized economy that included fishers, farmers, and merchants. Chincha elites acquired new power under Inca rule, but they were wealthy and politically powerful even before the empire reached their lands. They accumulated wealth through the trade and control of craft items (Alcalde et al. 2010), and probably exploited guano from offshore islands (Curatola 1997). They commanded large labor forces that created the abundant monumental mounds that currently dot the landscape. According to colonial accounts, exchanges occurred between coastal fishing communities and inland farmers who lived in economically specialized settlements (Rostworowski 1970).

At the Chincha capital of La Centinela, the Incas constructed a palace adjacent to the local ruler's residence and modified ritual sectors of the site (Morris and Santillana 2007), which included the oracle Chinchaycamac, a local creator considered to be a child of Pachacamac. Outside of La Centinela, the Incas built small storehouses, formalized road networks, and settled new sites, such as the fishing village Lo Demás (Sandweiss 1992). The Chincha reportedly managed long-distance trade to Ecuador under Inca rule, and Late Horizon burials in the valley contain artifacts and tools associated with trade, such as balances, blackware vessels, and *Spondylus* shell, some in the form of strands of red and white beads similar to *chaquira*. It is not known whether Chincha traders operated independently or as vassals of the Inca state, but they were an important arm of Inca wealth finance and operated as intermediaries with unincorporated groups in Ecuador. The Inca political economy in the valley focused on connecting coastal centers that oversaw farming and fishing, and possibly included more intensive exploitation of upper-valley copper mines. Social relationships with local elites, such as those who occupied the agricultural center of Las Huacas, were critical for implementing these changes. Inca and hybrid craft goods reinforced elite relationships (Dalton 2023), as did long-distance trade goods, which were used in new complex burial practices that emphasized ancestor veneration (Dalton et al. 2022).

The Chincha role in Inca-era maritime trade built the wealth and power of local elites while also increasing the flow of exotic goods to Cuzco. An important branch road entered the highlands in the neighboring Pisco Valley, passing through the local center of Lima la Vieja (Hyslop 1984) before reaching the *chaupi yunga* zone, where the Inca administrative center of Tambo Colorado and the extensive shrine site of Huaytará are located. From there, the road climbed and crossed the mountains, eventually joining the main Chinchaysuyu road to Cuzco at the highland center of Vilcashuamán.

Contisuyu Coast

To the south of the Nasca drainage, the Andes mountains run up almost all the way to the coastline, creating a limited desert pampa and foothills, and much smaller patches of alluvium that could be irrigated and cultivated. The coastal valleys at the edge of the Atacama Desert are typically drier than those to the north and had connections to Aymara-speaking groups living in the neighboring highlands, who used llama caravans to maintain agricultural colonies there in Inca times (Stanish 1989).

Along the coastline of the Contisuyu region, Inca strategies varied, and even when new centers were constructed, they interacted with local economies in different ways (Chacaltana 2015; Covey 2000). Overall, in this region Inca infrastructure was focused on establishing strategic movement across the region. At some sites, such as Camata Tambo, the Incas constructed storage features to accumulate staple goods (Figure 30), while at other sites, such as Quebrada Tacahuay, Inca-affiliated highlanders pursued a mix of farming, fishing, herding, and guano exploitation (Chacaltana 2015:315). Archaeological evidence indicates that the empire intensified existing exchange networks within and between coastal and highland regions, but the absence of large administrative sites suggests that Inca direct control over the region was minimal.

Conclusion

The Pacific coast was home to diverse polities that maintained distinct political economies. Some groups became Inca subjects after living under the centralized administration of the Chimú, whereas other groups entered the empire as autonomous polities. The Incas did not build new centers in the heavily settled coastal floodplains, and the strongest Inca presence in these littoral areas is at the Pachacamac shrine, where the Incas coopted and expanded the power of a local oracle to extend their own power and authority. Upvalley from local coastal centers, the Incas established administrative centers like Pueblo Viejo-Pukara, Tambo Colorado and Inkawasi in the *chaupi yunga*, where imperial officials could intensify and manage agricultural production and movement between the highlands and coast, some of it probably using the labor of resettled *mitimaes*. The Inca emphasis on *chaupi yunga* lands speaks to the economic plasticity of these mid-valley areas, which often had undeveloped economic

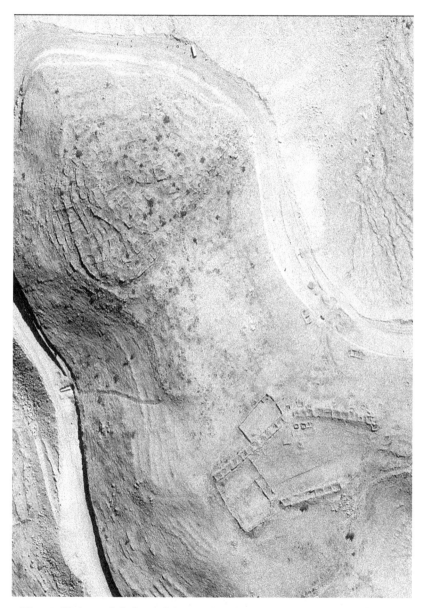

Figure 30 An aerial view of Camata Tambo and its associated settlement, located in the foothills of the south coast of Peru. The *tambo* was probably constructed to support strategic state movement across the zone, rather than financing state activities more broadly. Photo courtesy of Sofia Chacaltana.

potential when the Incas expanded onto the coast. Economic growth in these foothill areas largely supported imperial infrastructure, while also increasing the flow of wealth goods to Cuzco.

On the floodplains where there were already intensive and specialized economies, the Incas redirected the economic power of Chimú ruling elites by resettling artisans and supporting new long-distance trade patterns that involved coastal partners closer to Cuzco. The wealth seen in Inca-era coastal burials indicates that local elites played fundamental roles in the Inca manipulation of preexisting hierarchies and administrative infrastructure. Regionally, the empire built on preexisting physical infrastructure, such as craft production centers, canals, storage facilities, and roads. The Inca coastal road network developed existing roads and settlements strategically, so that the empire did not have to invest significantly in new construction. Storage and sites along the road supported movement across the network. Although storage was important and often associated with public areas, state storage facilities were much smaller than those in the central highlands. The Incas collected tribute of goods in kind (agricultural products, cloth), using *quipus* to record goods as they passed through the regional political economy. The coastal Inca political economy was dynamic and adapted to local considerations, but overall emphasized ritual patronage and road infrastructure, while investing less in the intensification of local staple economies. These investments helped to channel exotic raw materials toward Inca representatives who could use them in religious performances or send them to Cuzco to be transformed by Inca-affiliated artisans.

6 Imperial Economics in Marginal and Frontier Zones

Inca witnesses often appeared reluctant to acknowledge the wealth and power of coastal elites when describing their empire to the Spaniards, but they eagerly made claims about the supposed barbarity of Amazonian peoples living in the *yungas* to the east of the Andes. In 1571, while the Spanish viceroy Francisco de Toledo was in Cuzco, he assembled Andean *curacas* to testify about groups that the Incas had never conquered. Inca witnesses claimed that frontier groups like the Chunchos and Chiriguanaes were notorious cannibals, and that from time to time the Incas would give them convicted criminals to eat (Levillier 1940). This testimony echoed other early Inca accounts that portrayed groups living beyond imperial rule as savages who occupied landscapes that even the Incas could not civilize.

The theme of cultural and ecological foreignness that runs through the often-sketchy Inca accounts of frontier regions reflects social and political anxieties of an empire losing its expansionistic momentum, but it also speaks to economic practicalities developing along the frontiers. In the Cuzco region, the Incas shaped mountain valleys and channeled rivers for maize farming; in the tropical lowlands, they found people who used slash-and-burn techniques to cultivate unfamiliar foods, such as manioc and sweet potato. Lands beyond Inca control often contained desirable materials – colorful feathers, precious metals, and mind-altering plants – but highlanders struggled to acquire these things directly, whether in tropical rainforests, hyperarid deserts, or high mountain plateaus. Imperial frontiers overlapped with other regional exchange networks and Inca representatives engaged with well-connected people who could work on both sides of the frontier. While the empire suppressed trade and merchants in Cuzco and the highland provinces, it tolerated and even encouraged local traders who had the social contacts necessary to acquire exotic goods and raw materials that the Inca elite desired.

Although the Incas aspired to extend and intensify their administrative control and political economy, actual economic practices at the frontier zones varied. At the time of the Spanish invasion, Inca frontier and marginal zones surrounded the well-integrated highland provinces and included parts of present-day Ecuador and Colombia to the north (Figure 31), the Amazonian lowlands to the east, and the deserts and temperate uplands of Chile and northwest Argentina to the south (Figure 32). Across these areas, local and Inca strategies were still developing as the empire attempted to incorporate peripheries and exploit new populations and resources. Direct administration was not an inevitable outcome in these distant landscapes. In some places, Inca armies slowly ground out costly victories for decades, adding territory valley by valley in the face of determined resistance. In others, the Incas acknowledged that they were unwilling, or unable, to do so and embraced more indirect ways to maintain security and access exotic goods needed for wealth production.

Control and administration in these regions relied on strategic investments in lower-order state infrastructure, such as military garrisons, colonies, state farms, and craft workshops. These installations allowed Inca-affiliated people – and in some places, frontier traders – to acquire and move highly desired raw materials and worked craft items. These portable and valuable resources included metals, marine shells, gems, semiprecious stones, and feathers from exotic birds, all of which were used in Inca wealth production in Cuzco. In their attempts to monopolize the production and consumption of wealth flowing toward the capital, the Incas intervened selectively, allowing many local systems of craft production to continue, while at the same time exerting influence over long-distance trade routes and bottlenecks in important production processes. This included managing access to tin from Bolivia, an essential ingredient for producing their signature copper–tin bronze (Figure 33) (Earle 1994; Lechtman 1976), and overseeing the distribution of marine shells such as *Spondylus*.

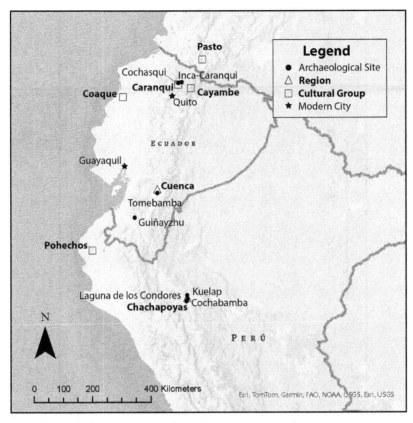

Figure 31 A map of the northeastern frontiers of the Inca Empire.

This section looks at the economic dynamics of three peripheral zones: (1) northern Chile/northwest Argentina, (2) the Amazonian lowlands, and (3) Ecuador and southern Colombia. Each region presented distinct economic opportunities and logistical costs based on local environments, existing economic practices, and the distribution of resources targeted by the Incas. For all their differences, these regions were all politically decentralized, requiring that the Incas negotiate with multiple leaders to navigate local politics. Within these interactions, imperial officials relied on local leaders and groups that were loyal to them, and often elevated the use of associated local styles. These groups often lacked the types of large-scale state infrastructure that the Incas needed, so they constructed what was considered necessary to maintain power. Building infrastructure at hardening frontiers encouraged different strategies than those used to consolidate control over inner provinces, where imperial infrastructure emphasized the rapid movement of troops, officials, and information out to the edge of the empire.

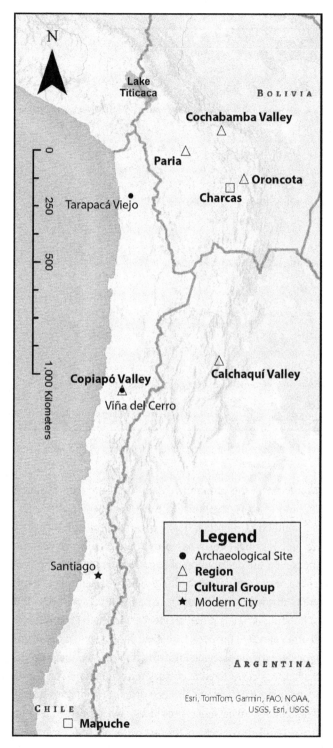

Figure 32 A map of the southeastern frontiers and marginal zones
of the Inca Empire.

Figure 33 A tin bronze *tumi* knife. Metropolitan Museum of Art
(1987.394.411).

The South

Although Andean researchers long believed the Incas made few conquests south of the Lake Titicaca Basin before the reign of Topa Inca Yupanqui, recent radiocarbon dates indicate an Inca presence in the distant southlands by around 1400 (Marsh et al. 2017). Inca expansion in Collasuyu eventually reached as far as the Maule River (central Chile), where the fierce resistance of Mapuche confederations repelled imperial soldiers. Prior to Inca expansion, groups in these regions maintained economic connections through established exchange routes that linked small coastal groups that specialized in marine hunting and fishing with groups that occupied different highland ecozones.

The southernmost parts of the Inca Empire contained many resources that were important for wealth production, including deposits of salt, copper, turquoise, and other lapidary materials. The Incas also promoted the use of copper–tin bronze, maintaining control by mediating access to tin sources in southern Bolivia. The Incas were motivated to extract these and other mineral resources that they transformed into prestige items that the Inca ruler and his representatives distributed, both as royal gifts and as ritual offerings. In addition to natural resources, they also gained access to a skilled labor force that had experience processing these items. At many sites, there is only evidence for certain stages of craft production, and Inca officials probably focused on overseeing the final stages of manufacturing, even if the initial stages occurred in largely decentralized networks (Garrido and Plaza 2020).

Groups in these regions were politically decentralized and the Incas had to negotiate with a variety of different local polities to incorporate existing infrastructure and construct new state-associated facilities (D'Altroy et al. 2000; Mignone 2023; Williams 2004). New state sites and enclaves were of modest size, and lacked large administrative palaces, *acllahuasi* compounds, and sun temples, suggesting a different mode of administration from what was established along the royal roads in the inner highland provinces. Strategic Inca infrastructure engaged with local settlements and long-distance caravan routes that operated prior to and during Inca expansion. Llamas were essential pack animals that transported goods along these trade routes, and while the Incas did not control all movement of goods along these paths, they promoted infrastructure that allowed them to alter the "rhythm and intensity of long-distance traffic" (Nielsen 2021:30). They constructed waystations that provided resources and fresh herds to allow caravans to travel more quickly. Whereas the Incas limited interregional trade in the central highlands by controlling the movement of people and goods – especially at bridges that crossed major rivers – in northern Chile, there is evidence that local caravans took advantage of Inca investments in infrastructure and increased non-state exchanges of lapidary and pigment products (Garrido 2016).

The most pronounced signs of Inca presence in southern Collasuyu are found in the highland and upper-valley regions, where they are strategically located near mineral resources, the primary Inca roads, and terraced fields where state colonists intensively farmed maize. In addition to economic investments in mining and agricultural colonization, the ceremonial engagement with powerful snowcapped mountains shaped imperial practices, channeling wealth goods and human sacrifices to places considered sacred to people living across the region. The disposal of rich offerings helped to establish Inca authority within local belief systems, and mountaintop shrines were often associated with forces that were believed to influence productive activities such as herding and mining.

Toward the southern end of the empire, the Incas incorporated Chile's Copiapó Valley, which offered access to extensive mineral deposits. Inca administration relied on relationships with local groups, such as the Diaguita. To mine and process these resources the Incas used local labor, as currently there is no strong evidence for *mitimaes* in the region. They did this by inserting their authority alongside mountaintop shrines and promoting distinct types of local material culture, including hybrid Diaguita–Inca wares. The exact types of hybrid wares varied between the coast and the highlands, underscoring how imperial officials navigated diverse local identities as they worked to build imperial power (Garrido 2018). At the mine of Viña del Cerro, the Incas built infrastructure to increase production of unalloyed copper, but the site and other Inca sites in the region lack clear evidence for the production of final metal artifacts. Regardless of the absence of evidence for local Inca production, copper–tin bronze artifacts do appear in local burials and were probably imported from another Inca province. Burials also include artifacts that are made from local alloys, demonstrating that the Inca preference for copper–tin bronze did not totally displace local traditions in this region (Garrido and Li 2017).

To the north, in the Quebrada Tarapacá, the Incas set up an administrative center at Tarapacá Viejo, which was well positioned at the center of multiple routes that connected the Atacama region. This meant that the Incas did not have to invest significant resources in creating roads and could utilize existing infrastructure (Zori et al. 2017). Differing from the Copiapó Valley, ethnohistoric sources note the presence of *mitimaes* from surrounding areas and fragments of a *quipu* were found at Tarapacá Viejo, which might have been a tool to manage labor and record tribute collected and stored at the site. The site contains evidence for multiple stages of metallurgical production, including the processing of ore, which occurred throughout the site and might indicate that local residents paid tribute in processed ore (Zori 2011). Outside of processing ore, there is evidence for the secondary refining and the production of finished metal artifacts, which differs sharply from the Copiapó Valley.

Moving southwest from Tarapacá, Argentina's Calchaquí Valley lies in the high *monte* ecozone of the eastern slopes of the Andes, where the Incas established new settlements or reoccupied previously abandoned sites (Figure 34). In this region, they often brought in *mitimaes* to work, increased regional agricultural production, and focused on strengthening social ties to groups that were friendly to them (D'Altroy et al. 2000; Mignone 2023; Williams 2004). Farming colonies were linked to imperial roads, minor storage depots, and residences for local elites who probably were representatives of the Inca state, all of which reflects a more limited state investment than is seen in the highland provinces closer to Cuzco. This difference in scale probably indicates that the Incas focused on wealth production rather than agricultural surplus and staple finance (Earle 1994). In Calchaquí, as well as throughout Collasuyu, the Incas gained access to extensive mineral resources that were turned into wealth items, but the available mortuary evidence suggests that very little of this wealth was distributed back into the community.

Figure 34 A photo of northwestern Argentina. From the Hyslop archive, courtesy of the Division of Anthropology, AMNH.

The Eastern Andean Slopes

To the east of the Andes lies the Amazon basin, a humid and densely vegetated lowland environment. On the eastern Andean slopes, the transitional high-altitude jungle ecozone known as the *ceja de selva* (eyebrow of the rainforest) was home to groups that interacted with both highlanders and peoples of the Amazon rainforest, who pursued different subsistence practices and spoke languages that were only distantly related to Quechua, Aymara, and other highland tongues. The Titicaca plateau in the south creates a broad expanse between the Amazon and the Pacific coast, but farther north the distance dividing the western and eastern slopes of the Andes becomes narrower. This means that while highland groups in the south-central Andes relied on long-distance caravans that traversed the high-altitude *puna* to engage in lowland exchanges, those living farther to the north had much more interaction with lowlanders throughout prehistory.

Currently, there is no evidence for Inca sites deep in the Amazonian lowlands. The lack of evidence for an Inca footprint in the Amazonian lowlands might be due to the limited archaeological research conducted in these inaccessible and overgrown landscapes. New discoveries could change our understanding of Inca expansion toward the east. For now, it appears that sites on the eastern Andean slopes served as strategic points where the Incas could develop connections with the Amazon and still use some of the agricultural technologies and administrative strategies developed in nearby highland valleys.

The Incas called the Amazonian lowlands the *yungas*, the term also used for the Pacific coast. Although both are lowland regions, there are major differences in the cultural identities and social organization of groups that inhabited them, as well as the natural resources found there. Amazonian groups were largely decentralized and possessed a high degree of genetic and linguistic diversity. Those that cultivated domesticated plants usually did so without extensive irrigation networks, instead using swidden ("slash and burn") techniques and the management of nutrient-rich soils to grow tubers (manioc, sweet potato), fruit and nut trees, and a diverse array of other plants. The Incas were not interested in producing the staple products that could be grown in the lowlands, but they were eager to obtain exotic materials not available in the highlands, including colorful bird feathers, jaguar pelts, tropical hardwoods, and herbs used in healing and rituals. The land on the eastern slope was also ideal for growing coca, a precious item that was deposited with ritual offerings and presented as an Inca gift used to build relationships with imperial subjects. Many of the rivers flowing from the Andes to the Amazon carried gold that could be panned out of alluvial deposits.

To acquire lowland resources such as coca and gold, the Incas established outposts and relationships in the higher-altitude *ceja de selva*. Where possible and necessary, they increased agricultural production by constructing terraces at elevations where they could grow maize, coca, and cotton (Bonavia 1968). As in the south in Argentina and Chile, Inca storage capacities were typically of modest scale, and the infrastructure probably supported the administrators and garrisons that occupied the Inca sites, and not the surrounding area (Snead 1992). A significant exception was the Cochabamba Valley in what is today Bolivia (Gyarmati and Condarco 2018). Campaigns under Topa Inca Yupanqui brought the valley under Inca control, leading to major imperial changes. The Incas initially focused on security, moving some of the local Chui and Cota population farther to the east to provide a buffer against the Guaraní-speaking lowland populations living beyond the frontier. A generation later, Huayna Capac transformed the Cochabamba Valley into a massive state farm that focused on maize production on a series of state fields. The agrarian overhaul of the valley floor established Inca lands (including some for the *mamacona* priestesses) that were worked by a population of highland *mitimaes* from the Titicaca Basin and Bolivian altiplano. The colonists received lands for their subsistence, and their native lords were granted maize lands to be worked for them. Permanent communities of Collas, Lupacas, Pacajes, and several other groups were joined seasonally by laborers

Figure 35 Photograph of excavated *collcas* at Kharalaus Pampa, Bolivia, a complex of circular and rectangular storehouses located at the edge of the Inca state farmlands in the Cochabamba Valley. Courtesy of János Gyarmati.

who helped with the harvest, some of whom brought llamas from state herds that they maintained for the Inca ruler.

The Incas built their largest storage complexes in this distant valley, and almost 2,500 structures have been identified in the Cochabamba Valley (Figure 35). Some of the maize grown there was used to feed soldiers who garrisoned nearby frontier forts, but significant quantities were packed into the highlands on llamas from Inca herds, which carried the harvest to the administrative center of Paria, and on to Cuzco. Huayna Capac's investment in large-scale maize intensification in the Cochabamba Valley was part of a broader economic development plan, which included moving existing populations from the valley into lower ecozones where high-yield production of coca leaf could be carried out (Julien 1998). Although Titicaca Basin elites gained greater access to maize by sending their people to work Inca lands in Cochabamba, they did not participate in the work of coca production.

Beyond the Cochabamba Valley, the Incas reported constant frustration with their southeastern border, where imperial campaigns made little headway against groups such as the Chiriguana and Charcas, who launched counter-attacks that threatened Inca subjects. Under Topa Inca Yupanqui and Huayna Capac, the Incas finally established militarized and fortified sites that were strong symbols of imperial power. In the region of Oroncota, located in

Figure 36 Double-jamb niches at the site of Oroncota. Photo courtesy of Sonia Alconini.

modern day Chuquisaca (Bolivia), the Incas established sites in the Pucara plateau that contained many of the hallmarks of Inca architecture, such as large double- and triple-jamb niches, and *kallankas* (Alconini 2008) (Figure 36). These structures with clear Inca architectural elements communicated close connections to the Inca ruler, but they were strategic outposts, and archaeological research has not recovered evidence that the Incas were able to enact major changes in settlement patterns or economic practices.

Prior to the Inca incursions, this area was occupied by the Yampara, Chicha, and Chui, who were part of the Charcas confederation (Alconini 2004:396), a network of highland Aymara herding groups and populations living in the valleys of the eastern Andean slopes. This coalition encompassed linguistic and stylistic differences, but there was intermarriage and exchange across cultural boundaries, which promoted political cohesion. Settlement patterns in the Oroncota region during the Late Horizon followed previous trends, where groups had increasingly focused on occupying the plateau rather than low-lying river areas. Furthermore, there is no evidence for the widespread use of imperial or hybrid Inca wares, nor other typical Inca prestige items that were part of the wealth finance system. While there is not much evidence of Inca material culture, pottery styles associated with lowland Amazonian groups are still found during the Inca period, showing continued connections with low-land groups under the Incas (Alconini 2013). Inca settlements in this region

Figure 37 A picture of the *ceja de selva*, or high montane rainforest. Photo from the Chachapoyas region by Lauren Pratt.

provided for immediate state needs and were not associated with major storage facilities.

Farther north, in the cloud forests of northern Peru (Figure 37), the Incas invested heavily in occupying the lands of the Chachapoyas, who fiercely resisted the military incursions of Topa Inca Yupanqui. After their defeat, large proportions of the Chachapoya population were taken to Cuzco as *yanacona* or were transplanted to distant provinces as *mitimaes*. Many of those resettled were posted on the highly contested northern frontier as more or less full-time solders (Murra 1986). Before conquest, the Chachapoyas were not a centralized state but rather a loose confederation of different ethnic groups. At first, the Incas administered them by establishing multiple state-affiliated centers such as the sites of Kuelap and Cochabamba (not to be confused with the site of Cochabamba in Bolivia) (Schjellerup 2015; Villar 2021). These centers did not have extensive storage capacity and were located along secondary routes connecting the central highlands to the Amazonian lowlands (Snead 1992:67–68). Although the Incas initially built multiple centers, it appears that over time Cochabamba became the main center.

As the empire resettled Chachapoya populations and built new state settlements, it imposed decimal administration onto local communities. The empire's ability to control local labor forces depended on the authority of local elites, whose changing identities can be seen in their burial practices (Buikstra and Nystrom 2015). One of the most impressive collections of *quipus* was recovered from Inca-era Chachapoya mummies at the site of Laguna de los Condores (Bjerregaard 2007). These *quipus* monitored populations and the labor of local groups that was part of Inca projects that sought to intensify the occupation of lowland areas where maize agriculture could be developed.

The North

When the first Spaniards reached the Inca world, the most contested border of the empire was the northern frontier, where Inca rulers campaigned for generations to conquer the independent chiefdoms of highland Ecuador and Colombia. Under Pachacuti Inca Yupanqui and Topa Inca Yupanqui, the Incas began integrating populations in the Ecuadorian highlands, and many sources credit Topa Inca Yupanqui with the decision to establish a heavily militarized royal center at Quito. The new construction projects associated with the intensifying Inca presence involved the transportation of andesite blocks from Cuzco quarries, more than 1,500 miles away (Ogburn 2004). This costly display showcased the Inca capacity to mobilize large labor forces for a construction project designed to communicate a close connection between Cuzco and distant provincial peoples.

Huayna Capac continued his predecessors' goals and worked to incorporate groups north of Quito and along the Ecuadorian coastline. The site of Tomebamba in Cuenca was probably the staging area for the northward expansion into the Caranqui, Cayambe, and Pasto territories (Salomon 2007[1986]). Inca campaigns gradually extended into northern Ecuador and southern Colombia, but the "front lines" were discontinuous, determined by topography and the force of local resistance. Rather than establishing far-flung outposts amidst local groups, the Incas incrementally extended a colonized territory where they established temples, garrisons, and palaces earlier on, and then introduced their own subjects as they moved to integrate local groups into the political economy. Many groups in the area resisted Inca expansion, such as the Caras (also known as the Caranquis), whose campaign against the Incas resulted in a bloody massacre where adult males were killed near a lake that came to be called Yahuarcocha, or "Blood Lake" in Quechua. This northward expansion was largely halted during the Inca civil war that broke out after Huayna Capac's death. During this conflict, Atahualpa claimed Quito as his seat of power, and he withdrew experienced soldiers from the frontier and sent them to invade the inner provinces and capture Cuzco in 1532.

As in other frontier zones, Inca expansion was motivated by access to exotic goods not abundantly available in the central highlands, such as gold and *Spondylus* shell. The Inca presence in Ecuador concentrated along the interior highlands, where the extension of the royal road helped to incorporate local chiefdoms into the empire and political economy. Following successful campaigns, the empire expanded maize agriculture and llama herding (Salomon 2007[1986]). The northern expansion was associated with different types of settlements. Some, such as Quito, were heavily militarized, whereas others included temples and administrative palaces. Tomebamba, the frontier seat of Huayna Capac's court, resembles Cuzco more closely than it does other provincial centers, such as Huánuco Pampa.

Inca nobles built fine architecture at Tomebamba, as well as many other sites in southern Ecuador (Figure 38), and burials there represent some of the only Inca-period tombs in the highlands in which gold adornments have been found (Flammang 2021). The southern part of highland Ecuador contains evidence for a wider integration of Quechua vocabulary, Inca religious customs, and Inca economic practices than those to the north in regions such as Pasto and Caranqui

Figure 38 Inca stonework from Cuenca. The Incas were working to establish a royal Inca center in Quito when the Spanish arrived in South America. Photo from the Hyslop archive, courtesy of the Division of Anthropology, AMNH.

(Bray 1992; Salomon 2007[1986]). At sites in southern Ecuador, such as Guiñayzhu in the Chilla mountains, the Incas constructed storehouses and intensified terraced agriculture (Jadán 2018), while at sites in the north, such as Inca-Caranqui and Cochasqui, they established ceremonial architecture and palaces. As this region was still in the process of being consolidated, it is possible that agricultural terraces and storehouses would have been built eventually, had Inca rule lasted longer.

Inca sites and constructions are found in the highlands, where, prior to the Incas, locals relied on what Frank Salomon refers to as a bizonal economy. In this system, leaders controlled the exchange and redistribution of resources between lowland maize-growing regions and the highland grazing area known as the *páramo*. The Incas sought to incorporate this preexisting system into their economic model (Salomon 2007[1986]:196), inserting themselves as key actors who bestowed rights to lands and herds. Such rights previously had been maintained through ancestral ties. As the Incas established themselves, local elites became dependent on Inca sovereignty to maintain their own claims, and many local groups that had been under Inca control for generations in southern Ecuador became close allies of the empire, as their own power and Inca power were closely aligned.

Groups in the Ecuadorian highlands also exchanged resources with the coast and the Amazon. These traders were known as *mindalaes* and were sponsored by local lords and sometimes traded using *chaquira* (Hechler 2021; Salomon 2007[1986]). On the coast, highland traders brought salt to trade for "gold, cotton, red pepper and dried fish" (Salomon 2007[1986]:105), as well as for *Spondylus* shell beads. With more salt, and the cotton, cloth, and gold that had been procured on the coast, traders who traveled to the eastern lowlands sought to acquire pigments, coca, mind-altering drugs, and ritual knowledge, in addition to this exchange of resources across the environmental zones.

While in parts of the Inca Empire, including the highlands of Ecuador, the Incas restricted trade and movement, there is evidence that *mindalaes* and other types of traders were allowed to continue under Inca rule. This is probably because these traders acquired marine shell and metals that the Incas could not otherwise access directly in their highland territories. On the Ecuadorian coast, the vertical trade routes of the *mindalaes* intersected with the maritime trade along the coast, which favored the Chincha and other polities of the south and central coast during the period of Inca rule (see Section 5). Coastal traders from Chincha and other valleys appear to have exchanged quantities of highly valuable goods and raw materials, which would explain the large collection of balances (scales) from the Chincha Valley (Figure 39).

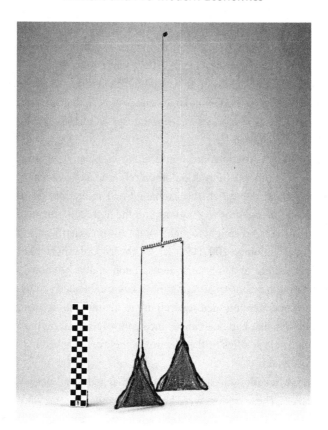

Figure 39 Along the Andean coast balances were used from AD 1200 into the colonial period to weigh small amounts of coca, cotton, and metal. (Photo courtesy of the Division of Anthropology, AMNH. 41.2/8987.)

During the early colonial period in Ecuador and Colombia, balances were associated with the Pasto and Coaque areas, where they were used to weigh small amounts of metal (Estete 1924). Balances have also been found along the Peruvian coast and date as far back as approximately AD 1200 (Dalton 2024). Due to the low density of this artifact type in most archaeological assemblages – and the long-held assumption that trade was limited everywhere in the Inca-era Andes – the use of balances to measure quantities of valuable trade goods has not been integrated into an understanding of Andean commercial and political economies. Based on current studies, the highest density of these items has been recovered from the central and south coasts, in regions such as the Rímac, Chincha, and Ica Valleys. Balances are typically between 5 and 20 cm long and would have been used to weigh small quantities of valuable goods, such as coca, cotton, and metals. While details surrounding the use of balances remain unclear, analyses of the artifacts demonstrate that they served multiple purposes and were used to weigh a variety of goods.

For the Incas, the Ecuadorian coast presented opportunities to acquire valuable goods that could fuel their wealth economy. They reached the Ecuadorian coast toward the end of a long period of dynamic change known as the Integration Period (AD 800–1532). During this period, populations grew, and groups became more centralized and hierarchical. Sites also became more densely populated, and alongside a broader emphasis on trade and exchange, groups developed stronger connections with northern Peru. Local populations relied on kin structures for political authority and production was organized at the household level (Martin 2010). Shell beads (*chaquira*) and metal artifacts began to be used in the long-distance exchanges of valuable goods. These metal artifacts included ingots or sheet metal (*chipana*), pieces of hammered copper (known as *naipes*), so-called "axe-monies," and polished gold buttons (*chagualas*) (Figure 40). Spanish eyewitnesses described stores of ingots in Cuzco, and the chronicler Santillán (1879[1563:#51]) later stated that some coastal populations used *chipanas* and metal bangles to pay their tribute to the Incas. *Naipes* are I-shaped sheets of arsenical copper that were produced in northern Peru during the Middle Sicán Period (AD 900–1100) and are found associated with contemporary Manteño populations in Ecuador. *Naipes* were probably traded by the Sicán polity to the Manteños for *Spondylus*. In Ecuador, they served as a medium of exchange and in the Sicán region were a prestige item that represented control over resources and labor (Shimada and Merkle 2021). Manteño graves are also associated with metal artifacts that have been referred to as "axe-monies." While these items remain poorly understood, current research on the weight distribution of axe-monies has not found evidence that they were weight-regulated and conclude that they were likely ingots whose value derived from their ability to be reworked into new prestige items (Montalvo-Puente et al. 2023).

Many parts of coastal Ecuador were never formally integrated into the Inca Empire, and the presence of exchange media such as *naipes* and *chagualas*, which were used in Colombia and regions farther to the north, attests to the region's role as an economic crossroads. In these areas there is no indication of the same type of Inca footprint as seen in the highlands, which included increased agricultural production. Nor is there evidence for the establishment of Inca ritual centers like those seen at Cochasqui and Inca-Caranqui. Nevertheless, coastal groups provided access to highly desired goods, and a diverse array of traders played essential roles in acquiring and moving these resources. On the Amazonian slopes of Ecuador, Inca expansion also varied from the typical highland model. As is the case farther south in the Peruvian and Bolivian

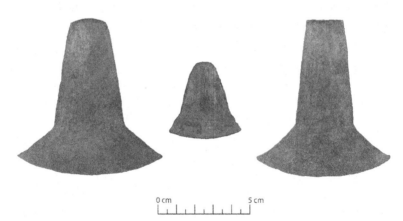

Figure 40 Photos of *naipes* (top) and axe-monies (bottom), courtesy of Izumi Shimada and Carlos Montalvo-Puente, respectively.

Amazon, there is no evidence for direct Inca expansion and settlements in the Amazon, even though the region provided access to important resources like colorful feathers and plants that were important in shamanic rituals.

Craft production in Ecuador was largely decentralized prior to the Incas, and on the coast it was managed at the household level. Research in the Caranqui region indicates that the Incas reorganized local production to weaken horizontal relationships between groups (Bray 1992). While the Incas did insert themselves into the local production network, geochemical and petrographic analysis demonstrates that pottery production was less regulated in Ecuador than in the Inca heartland (Bray and Minc 2020). Production of *Spondylus* shell beads and metal artifacts was probably conducted partially, if not entirely, outside of Inca control. In contrast, there is evidence that the Incas were more involved in the production of obsidian artifacts in the highlands, as compositional analysis of obsidian demonstrates that the raw material for those artifacts originated within the Inca Empire, rather than sources beyond the frontier (Ogburn et al. 2009).

Conclusion

The Inca frontiers and marginal zones described in this section demonstrate the dynamic nature of Inca political economy, and the diverse ways that the Incas engaged with distant and unfamiliar landscapes and peoples to build economic power. Across all frontiers, the Incas restricted much of their intervention to highland areas, especially those where they could establish valley-bottom terraced agriculture and introduce elements of the administrative strategies developed in the central highlands. In some regions, such as the Chachapoyas, they sought to control labor and promoted new mortuary practices to bring groups into the empire. In other regions, such as the northern Calchaquí Valley, they founded new sites and installed only the infrastructure needed to support *mitimaes* and administrators sent to live there.

At each of the frontiers discussed in this section, state officials confronted distinct new challenges, and they developed strategies that reflected varying degrees of economic plasticity as they intertwined their political economy with preexisting practices. In the south, the empire developed trade networks for caravans, creating waystations and storehouses that allowed groups to move faster along state-monitored routes. In the north, they carefully integrated their own sovereignty into that of local elites, who quickly became dependent on them for access to land and herds. Like the long-distance caravan drivers of the south-central Andes, the maritime and overland traders of the Ecuadorian coast carried out interregional transactions that were not common in the central highlands. The exchanges on the northern frontiers employed an array of worked goods – shell beads, cloth, metal objects – as mediums of exchange, a reflection of their economic intersections with populations living along the Pacific coast and in the northern Andes. Frontier exchanges persisted during Inca efforts to expand and consolidate their control, but the empire does not seem to have attempted to incorporate these practices in other provinces by promoting long-distance caravan trade or the use of new exchange media at a broad scale. Although new research in the coming years will undoubtedly enhance our understandings of the economic relationships that developed along

Inca frontiers, it is clear that economic life at the edges of the Inca world varied substantially during the generations of imperial growth and intensification.

7 Conclusion

This *Element* has combined archaeological and ethnohistoric data to describe how the Inca political economy engaged with the diverse subsistence and exchange practices of different Andean regions. The synthesis of multiple lines of evidence helps to recast some of the misrepresentations of Andean economics that appeared in colonial chronicles and secondary literature. Although many questions remain, recent scholarship highlights the importance of integrating regional studies into a broader picture of Inca administration, updating earlier work on Inca provincial chronologies, infrastructural invest-ments, and economic intensification. New data from surveys and excavations will help to identify more nuanced economic patterns, particularly through the accumulation of radiocarbon dates and archaeometric analyses of metal arti-facts, ceramics, and textiles. New data are needed to quantify the scale of wealth production and its social distribution across the empire. As scholars study the different ways that individuals accumulated and displayed wealth across the Andes, it will be important to consider the extent to which wealth produced within the empire was traded beyond imperial frontiers, where ordinary Inca goods might become exotic status goods.

For now, the available evidence makes it possible to identify some general patterns and processes that influenced how the Inca political economy mani-fested within changing local systems. In the Cuzco region, the Inca nobility used tributary labor and special social statuses to create productive landscapes and generate vast amounts of wealth. Accounts of Inca Cuzco describe how gener-ations of Inca royals increased their control over improved lands, skilled labor, and valuable raw materials as they promoted their city as the center of the Andean world. The wealth of Cuzco differs substantially from the surrounding central highlands, where even elites closely aligned with the Incas did not have access to many wealth items. In those directly administered provinces, Inca subjects labored to build infrastructure, extend and hold imperial frontiers, and produce the staple and wealth goods that funded local administration and elevated Cuzco over other parts of the Andes. The three highland provinces discussed in Section 4 indicate considerable differences in the implementation of Inca economic policies.

The relative scarcity of personal wealth in the highlands contrasts sharply with the Peruvian coast prior to and during Inca rule. Coastal societies main-tained highly productive economies based on intensive agriculture and fishing.

Urbanization, economic specialization, and long-distance exchange were well-developed before the Incas extended their indirect rule over the coast, and they persisted under Inca rule in ways that were distinct from the central highlands. At the frontiers, Inca soldiers, colonists, and officials engaged with even more diverse groups that had different kinds of political leadership and economic exchange practices. Many of these decentralized regions were still being contested when the Spanish invaded and colonized the Andean world, but in some places the Incas were content to focus on frontier security and maintain economic exchanges with independent groups and specialized traders rather than attempting to impose direct administration. Overall, the economic practices found across distant provinces varied considerably, reflecting an Inca focus on targeting places with higher degrees of economic plasticity, especially those where new staple production could fund infrastructure and wealth production. In places where highland staple practices offered more limited prospects of economic growth, they tended to work through local elites and traders to try and redirect raw materials and wealth goods into Inca-controlled networks.

The strategies and footprint of Inca administration looked different in different areas. In the Sacred Valley, Inca expansion took the form of royal estates and terracing, while in sites adjacent to the ocean, Inca architectural elements focused on locally sacred places, such as the Sun Temple at Pachacamac. Inca occupation is also associated with hybrid styles used to reflect both Inca and local authority. What it meant to be "Inca" – or not – clearly varied from place to place in the Andes. Similarly, Inca administrative tools are not uniformly distributed throughout the empire. Regardless of preservation bias, artifacts such as *quipus, yupanas,* and balances are more common in certain areas than others, raising questions about how counting, weighing, and record-keeping supported different administrative and economic strategies. These economic practices were more than a modest extension of *ayllu* practices, and researchers are increasingly reconsidering assumptions of economic self-sufficiency within highland *ayllus* and bringing attention to how staple and wealth goods might have circulated outside of kin-based practices of reciprocity and redistribution.

Inca Economics in Comparative Context

Although the Inca case is distinctive in many regards, it offers some points of comparison with other early empires that can inform the broader study of ancient political economies. Like Rome and Tenochtitlán (the Aztec capital), Cuzco grew into a cosmopolitan capital where wealth from the provinces was concentrated and used in lavish displays. As the Roman and Aztec Empires expanded, the economic role of markets and commerce increased in core regions (albeit in different ways), something that did not occur in Cuzco or nearby highland provinces. The Inca suppression of commerce and conventional wealth finance might be explained as a result of the economic circumstances under which Inca highland campaigns occurred. In mountain valleys where local populations focused on low-surplus subsistence strategies, the Incas had to increase staple surpluses, build infrastructure, and sponsor the production of wealth goods that would reinforce imperial social hierarchies.

The Inca system of labor taxation also helped to limit the development of regional commerce, since provincial administration could be maintained largely by dispensing local staple and craft goods. Even *camayos*, from garrison soldiers to silversmiths to low-order administrators, were granted lands to work for their subsistence – there was no need to pay them money for their services to the Inca. Festivals of celebratory reciprocity drew on the same stores of staple goods used to provision state workers. The emphasis on staple production might explain the limited development of urbanization in the Inca-era highlands, which contrasts with the demographic changes occurring in the Aztec and Roman worlds.

As provincial staple economies developed to maintain military and political activities, the Inca ideology of sovereign ritual performance promoted sumptuary rules that kept wealth out of the homes and tombs of all but the highest-ranking elites in the central highlands, limiting potential for commercial development. Under the Incas, some groups on the coast and in periphery and frontier regions experienced an increase in access to local and long-distance trade goods, but most regions did not see significant changes in domestic economy or wealth consumption following their incorporation into the Inca Empire, unlike populations in many Roman and Aztec provinces.

Elites in the Roman, Aztec, and Inca empires sought to increase their access to luxury goods by expanding their territories, and they relied on traders to acquire valuables coming from beyond their domains. Although much has been made of the absence of coinage in the Inca world, the identification of regionally traded exchange media (e.g., *chaquira*, axe-monies) blurs some of the contrast with other empires, especially given that they often used non-metal exchange media for long-distance trade. Aztec markets used cotton cloth and cacao beans as currency, and Roman traders operating beyond the imperial frontiers bartered a range of valuables, including textiles, metalwork, glassware, and gold coins that were valuable for their metal weight. Similar objects circulated at the margins of the Inca world and in the broader trade networks that overlapped with some Inca frontiers. It is worth noting that trade in all three empires flourished in places where low-cost movement was possible. The Mediterranean Sea and Basin of Mexico were both associated with the development of sophisticated commercial networks. The Pacific maritime trade that flourished in coastal Andean regions only indirectly benefited the Inca political economy.

The economies of the Inca world were diverse and dynamic, and Inca political economy developed with an eye to the perceived costs and opportunities to be derived from local landscapes and societies. Although Andean ecology and social values set the Inca case apart from other early empires, the rich evidence on infrastructural development, staple finance, and administrative flexibility raises questions of interest in other world regions. The state reliance on an idiom of kin-based reciprocity offers an alternative to the commercial, institutionalized, and bureaucratic practices that many scholars assume were necessary to build and maintain power in ancient states.

Glossary

Note: Where possible, Quechua terms reflect orthography and translated definitions found in the earliest surviving dictionary (Santo Tomás 1560). Many Quechua nouns appear in the chronicles in the plural form, indicated by the ending *-cona*.

aclla/acllacona (Quechua): a girl selected for gendered training in the *acllahuasi*.

acllahuasi (Q.): "house of the chosen," a female enclosure managed by the *mamacona*.

Antisuyu (Q.): one of the major Inca provinces (*suyu*), associated with the Amazonian lowlands.

apu (Q.): great lord.

ayllu (Q.): lineage or family.

ayni (Q.): reciprocity.

cacay (Q.): sales tax or tribute.

cacique (Taíno): hereditary local leader.

camayo/camayoc: skilled producer (e.g., cocacamayo, queroscamayo).

capac (Q.): king.

capacocha (Q.): Inca child sacrifice.

catu/cato (Q.): barter marketplace.

ceja de selva (Spanish): cloud forest zone of Amazonian slope.

chacara (Q.): estate, property, agricultural plot.

chasqui (Q.): an Inca message-runner.

chaguala (unknown): gold "buttons" traded in Colombian highlands.

chani (Q.): value.

chapa (Q.): estate, property, agricultural plot.

chapi (Q.): luxury good.

chaquira (Kuna?): strands of small red shell beads, typically *Spondylus*.

charqui (Q.): dried meat.

chaupi yunga (Q): coastal Andean foothill zone.

chuño (Q.): freeze-dried potatoes.

Chinchaysuyu (Q.): one of the major Inca provinces (*suyu*), encompassing lands northwest of Cuzco.

chipana (Q.): metal sheet.

ciudadela (Spanish): common name used for royal Chimú palace compounds at Chan Chan.

Collasuyu (Q.): one of the major Inca provinces (*suyu*), including the Titicaca Basin and south-central Andes.

collca (Q.): storehouse.

Contisuyu (Q.): one of the major Inca provinces (*suyu*), corresponding to territory to the south of Cuzco.

Coya (Q.): paramount female Inca title.

curaca (Q.): principal lord.

encomienda (Sp.): grant of Indigenous labor to a Spaniard (*encomendero*) responsible for providing Christian instruction.

guaccha (Q.): poor, without kin.

hacienda (Sp.): country estate.

hanan (Q.): "upper," used to distinguish the descendants of the last six Incas (Hanan Cuzco).

huaca (Q.): sacred or supernatural being or place.

hunu (Q.): 10,000, the household count for an ideal Inca province.

huaranca (Q.): 1,000.

hurin (Q.): "lower," used to distinguish the descendants of the first five Incas (Hurin Cuzco).

kallanka (Q.): common name referring to elongated Inca great halls.

mama/mamacona (Q.): "mother(s)," title of trained Inca religious women.

mindalá (Q.): status merchant operating along the northern Inca frontier.

mit'a (Q.): Indigenous Andean rotational community service.

mita (Q.): compulsory labor service imposed by Spanish officials on Andean tributary populations.

mitima/mitimaes (Q.): Inca-resettled labor colonist.

monte (Sp.): a high, arid ecozone characterized by wide-ranging and often low temperatures.

naipe (Sp.): common name referring to "axe moneys" found in northern Peru and Ecuador.

pachaca (Q.): 100.

panaca (Q.): a royal kin group comprising the descendants of an Inca and Coya.

páramo (Sp.): a high, marginal plateau ecozone.

piñasni (Q.): debt.

pirhua (Q.): storage bin.

pucara (Q.): hilltop fortress.

puna (Q.): zone of high-elevation grasslands.

quipu (Q.): Andean record-keeping system that uses knotted cords, maintained by specialists (*quipucamayo*).

randini (Q.): trade

Sapa Inca (Q.): paramount male Inca title.

sayua (Q.): boundary marker.

sinche/sinchecona (Q.): general term used to describe highland pre-Inca war leaders.

suyu (Q.): division of land.

tambo (Q.): waystation.

tarwi (Q.): *Lupinus mutabilis*, a member of the lupin family cultivated for its high-protein beans.

tasa (Sp.): annual levy of tribute, divided into specified categories.

Tawantinsuyu (Q.): "The Four Parts Together," the vernacular name for the Inca Empire.

tumi (Q.): metal axe.

yana/yanacona (Q.): servant in a royal household, often taken from a resistant Inca province.

yayanc (Q.): lord, master.

yma ayca (Q.): abundance.

yunga (Q.): lowlands, either the Pacific coast or Amazonian basin.

yupana (Q.): a device, often carved of stone, used with counting tokens (stones, beans) to perform calculations.

References

Alcalde Gonzáles, J., del Águila Chávez, C., Fujita Alarcón, F., & E. Retamozo Rondón. (2010). "Plateros" precoloniales tardíos en Tambo de Mora, valle de Chincha (siglos XIV–XVI). *Arqueología y Sociedad*, **21**, 171–184.

Alconini, S. (2004). The Southeastern Inka frontier against the Chiriguanos: structure and dynamics of the Inka imperial borderlands. *Latin American Antiquity* **15**(4), 389–418.

Alconini, S. (2008). Dis-embedded centers and architecture of power in the fringes of the Inka Empire: new perspectives on territorial and hegemonic strategies of domination. *Journal of Anthropological Archaeology* **27**(1), 63–81.

Alconini, S. (2013). El Territorio Kallawaya y el taller alfarero de Milliraya: evaluación de la producción, distribución e intercambio interregional de la cerámica Inka provincial. *Chungara, Revista de Antropología Chilena* **45**(2), 277–292.

Arkush, E. (2010). *Hillforts of the Ancient Andes: Colla Warfare, Society, and Landscape*. Gainesville: University Press of Florida.

Barraza Lescano, S., Areche Espinola, R., & G. Marcone. (2022). By stones and by knots: the counting and recording of chili peppers stored during the Inca occupation of the Guarco administrative center of Huacones-Vilcahuasi, lower Canete Valley, Peru. *Andean Past* **13**, 221–264.

Bauer, B. (1992). *The Development of the Inca State*. Austin: University of Texas Press.

Bauer, B. (2004). *Ancient Cuzco: Heartland of the Inca*. Austin: University of Texas Press.

Bauer, B., & C. Stanish. (2001). *Ritual and Pilgrimage in the Ancient Andes: The Islands of the Sun and the Moon*. Austin: University of Texas Press.

Bauer, B., Aráoz Silva, M., & T. Hardy. (2022). The settlement history of the Lucre Basin (Cusco, Peru). *Andean Past* **13**, 149–192.

Betanzos, J. de. (1996[1550s]). *Narrative of the Incas*. Tr. Roland Hamilton. Austin: University of Texas Press.

Bjerregaard, L., & A. von Hagen. (2007). *Chachapoya Textiles: The Laguna de los Condores Textiles in the Museo Leymebamba, Chachapoyas, Perú*. Copenhagen: Museum Tusculanum Press.

Bonavia, D. (1968). *Las ruinas del Abiseo*. Lima: CONCYT.

Bray, T. (1992). Archaeological survey in northern highland Ecuador: Inca imperialism and the Pais Caranqui. *World Archaeology* **24**(2), 218–233.

Bray, T., & J. Echeverría. (2018). The Inca centers of Tomebamba and Caranqui in northern Chinchaysuyu. In S. Alconini and R. A. Covey, eds., *The Oxford Handbook on the Incas*, pp. 159–178. Oxford: Oxford University Press.

Bray, T., & L. Minc. (2020). The imperial Inca-style pottery from Ecuador: insights into provenance and production using INAA and ceramic petrography. *Journal of Archaeological Science: Report* **34**, 102628.

Buikstra, J., & K. Nystrom. (2015). Ancestors and social memory: a South American example of dead body politics. In I. Shimada and J. Fitzsimmons, eds., *Living with the Dead in the Andes*, pp. 245–266. Tucson: University of Arizona Press.

Canziani Amico, J. (2012). *Ciudad y territorio en los Andes: contribuciones a la historia del urbanismo prehispánico*. Lima: Fondo Editorial de la Pontificia Universidad Católica del Perú.

Carter, Benjamin P. (2011). Spondylus in South American prehistory. In F. Ifantidis and M. Nikolaidou, eds., *Spondylus in Prehistory: New Data and Approaches. Contributions to the Archaeology of Shell Technologies*, pp. 63–89. Oxford: Archaeopress.

Castro, C., & D. de Ortega Morejón. (1938[1558]). Relaçion y declaraçion del modo que este valle de chincha y sus comarcanos se governavan Antes que / oviese yngas y despues q(ue) los vuo hasta q(ue) los (christian)os e(n)traron en esta tierra. In H. Trimborn, ed., *Quellen zur Kulturgeschichte des präkolumbinischen Amerika*, pp. 217–262. Stuttgart: Strecker und Schröder.

Chacaltana Cortez, S. (2015). Regional Interfaces between Inca and Local Communities in the Colesuyo Region of Southern Peru. PhD dissertation, University of Illinois, Chicago.

Chacaltana Cortez, S., Baca Marroquín, E., Hernández Garavito. C., Norman, S., & M. E. Grávalos. (2023). Inka and local ceramic production and distribution networks: a view from the Chinchaysuyu and Colesuyo. *Journal of Archaeological Science: Reports* **48**, 103910.

Cieza de León, P. de. (1984[1553]). *La crónica del Perú*. Ed. Manuel Ballesteros. Madrid: Historia 16.

Cieza de León, P. de. (1880[c. 1553]). *Segunda parte de la Crónica del Perú*. Ed. Marcos Jiménez de la Espada. Madrid: Manuel Ginés Hernández.

Cobo, B. (1892[1653]). *Historia del nuevo mundo*, tomo III. Ed. Marcos Jiménez de la Espada. Seville: Imp. E. Rasco.

Conklin, W. (1982). The information system of Middle Horizon quipus. *Annals of the New York Academy of Sciences* **385**(1), 261–281.

Costin, C., & T. Earle. (1989). Status distinction and legitimation of power as reflected in changing patterns of consumption in late prehispanic Peru. *American Antiquity* **54**(4), 691–714.

Covey, R. A. (2000). Inka administration of the far south coast of Peru. *Latin American Antiquity* **11**(2), 119–138.

Covey, R. A. (2006). *How the Incas Built Their Heartland: State Formation and the Innovation of Imperial Strategies in the Sacred Valley, Peru.* Ann Arbor: University of Michigan Press.

Covey, R. A., ed. (2014). *Regional Archaeology in the Inca Heartland: The Hanan Cuzco Surveys.* Ann Arbor: University of Michigan Museum of Anthropological Archaeology.

Covey, R. A. (2015). Kinship and the Inca imperial core: multiscalar archaeological patterns in the Sacred Valley (Cuzco, Peru). *Journal of Anthropological Archaeology* **40**, 183–195.

Covey, R. A. (2018). Archaeology and Inka origins. *Journal of Archaeological Research* **26**, 253–304.

Covey, R. A., & D. Amado Gonzáles, eds. (2008). *Imperial Transformations in Sixteenth-Century Yucay, Peru.* Ann Arbor: University of Michigan Museum of Anthropology.

Covey, R. A., Bauer, B., Bélisle, V., & L. Tsesmeli. (2013). Regional perspectives on Wari state influence in Cusco, Peru (c. AD 600–1000). *Journal of Anthropological Archaeology* **32**(4), 538–552.

Covey, R. A., Quave, K., & C. Covey. (2016). Inka storage systems in the imperial heartland (Cusco, Peru): risk management, economic growth, and political economy. In L. Manzanilla and M. Rothman, eds., *Storage in Ancient Complex Societies: Administration, Organization, and Control*, pp. 167–188. Walnut Creek: Left Coast Press.

Curatola, M. (1997). Guano: una hipótesis sobre el origen de la riqueza del señorío de Chincha. In R. Varón and J. Flores, eds., *Arqueología, Antropología, e Historia En Los Andes: Homenaje a María Rostworowski*, pp. 223–239. Lima: Instituto de Estudios Peruanos.

Dalton, J. (2020). Excavations at Las Huacas (AD 1200–1650): Exploring Elite Strategies and Economic Exchange during the Inca Empire. PhD dissertation, University of Michigan.

Dalton, J. (2023). Hybrid material culture in the Inca Empire (AD 1400–1532): analyzing the ceramic assemblages from La Centinela and Las Huacas, Chincha Valley. *Latin American Antiquity* 1–19. doi:10.1017/laq.2023.21.

Dalton, J. (2024). The Use of Balances in Late Andean Prehistory. *Cambridge Archaeological Journal FirstView*, 1–20. DOI: https://doi.org/10.1017/S0959774324000076.

Dalton, J., Gómez Mejía, J., Oncebay Pizarro, N., Tomažič, I., & E. Cobb. (2022). The dead do not unbury themselves: understanding posthumous engagement and ancestor veneration in coastal Peru (AD 1450–1650). *Journal of Anthropological Archaeology* **66**, 101410.

D'Altroy, T. (2014). *The Incas, 2nd edition*. New York: Blackwell.

D'Altroy, T., & C. Hastorf. (1984). The distribution and contents of Inca state storehouses in the Xauxa region of Peru. *American Antiquity* **49**(2), 334–349.

D'Altroy, T., & C. Hastorf, eds. (2001). *Empire and Domestic Economy*. New York: Springer.

D'Altroy, T. N., & T. K. Earle (1985). Staple finance, wealth finance, and storage in the Inka political economy. *Current Anthropology* **26**(2), 187–197.

D'Altroy, T., Lorandi, A. M., Williams, V., *et al*. (2000). Inka rule in the Northern Calchaqui Valley, Argentina. *Journal of Field Archaeology* **27**(1), 1–26.

Davenport, J. (2020). The organization of production for Inka polychrome pottery from Pachacamac, Peru. *Journal of Anthropological Archaeology* **60**, 101235.

Delaere, C., & J. Capriles. (2020). The context and meaning of an intact Inca underwater offering from Lake Titicaca. *Antiquity* **94**(376), 1030–1041.

Delgado González, C. (2013). Feasts and offerings in Arcopata, Cusco. *Andean Past* **11**, 85–110.

Delgado González, C. (2014). La ocupación Inca en Conventomoqo, Valle del Cusco. *Arqueología y Sociedad* **27**, 95–110.

Diez de San Miguel, G. (1964[1567]). *Visita hecha a la provincia de Chucuito por Garci Díez de San Miguel en el año 1567*. Ed. John Murra. Lima: Ediciones de la Casa de la Cultura.

Dillehay, T. (1977). Tawantinsuyu integration of the Chillon Valley, Peru: a case of Inca geo-political mastery. *Journal of Field Archaeology* **4**(4), 397–405.

Earle, T. (1994). Wealth finance in the Inka Empire: evidence from the Calchaqui Valley, Argentina. *American Antiquity* **59**(3), 443–460.

Eeckhout, P. (2012). Inca storage and accounting facilities at Pachacamac. *Andean Past* **10**, 213–239.

Eeckhout, P., & E. López-Hurtado. (2018). Pachacamac and the Inca on the coast of Peru. In S. Alconini and R. A. Covey, eds., *The Oxford Handbook on the Incas*, pp. 179–196. Oxford: Oxford University Press.

Espinoza Soriano, W. (1971). Los Huancas, aliados de la Conquista: tres informaciones inéditas sobre la participación indígena en la conquista del Perú 1558, 1560, 1561. *Anales científicos, Universidad Nacional del Centro del Perú* **1**, 9–407.

Espinoza Soriano, W. (1974). El habitat de la etnía Pinagua, siglos XV y XVI. *Revista del Museo Nacional* **40**, 157–220.

Espinoza Soriano, W. (1976). Las mujeres secundarias de Huayna Capac. Dos casos de señoralismo feudal en el Imperio Inca. *Revista del Museo Nacional* **42**, 247–298.

Estete, M. de. (1924). Relación que del descubrimiento y conquista del Perú hizo el capitán Miguel de Estete al Supremo Consejo de las Indias. *Colección de Libros y Documentos Referentes a La Historia Del Perú* **8**, 3–56.

Flammang, A. (2021). Inca funerary practices (c. 1400–1532): a first assessment on the basis of archaeological data. *Ñawpa Pacha* **42**(2), 261–286.

Garcilaso de la Vega, "El Inca." (1609). *Primera parte de los comentarios reales que tratan del origen de los Yncas, reyes que fueron del Perú ...* Lisbon: Pedro Crasbeeck.

Garrido, F. (2016). Rethinking imperial infrastructure: a bottom-up perspective on the Inca road. *Journal of Anthropological Archaeology* **43**, 94–109.

Garrido Escobar, F. (2018). Los nuevos sujetos imperiales del valle de Copiapó: estilos Diaguita e Inca local en los pucos del período Tardío. *Estudios atacameños*: **60**, 51–76.

Garrido, F., & M. T. Plaza. (2020). Provincial Inca metallurgy in northern Chile: new data for the Viña del Cerro smelting site. *Journal of Archaeological Science: Reports* **33**, 102556.

Garrido, F., & T. Li. (2017). A handheld XRF study of Late Horizon metal artifacts: implications for technological choices and political intervention in Copiapó, Northern Chile. *Archaeological and Anthropological Sciences* **9**, 935–942.

Gordon, R., & R. Knopf. (2007). Late Horizon silver, copper, and tin from Machu Picchu, Peru. *Journal of Archaeological Science* **34**(1), 38–47.

Gyarmati, J., & C. Condarco. (2018). Inca imperial strategies and installations in central Bolivia. In S. Alconini and R. A. Covey, eds., *The Oxford Handbook of the Incas*, pp. 119–136. New York: Oxford University Press.

Hayashida, F. (1999). Style, technology, and state production: Inka pottery manufacture in the Leche Valley, Peru. *Latin American Antiquity* **10**(4), 337–352.

Hechler, R. (2021). Over the Andes and through their foods: late pre-Columbian political economic relations in northern Ecuador. In R. Clasby and J. Nesbitt, eds., *The Archaeology of the Upper Amazon: Complexity and Interaction in the Andean Tropical Forest*, pp. 208–227. Gainesville: University of Florida Press.

Hirth, K., & J. Pillsbury. (2013). Redistribution and markets in Andean South America. *Current Anthropology* **54**(5), 642–647.

Hu, D., & K. Quave. (2020). Prosperity and Prestige: Archaeological Realities of Unfree Laborers under Inka Imperialism. *Journal of Anthropological Archaeology* **59**, 101201.

Hyslop, J. (1984). *The Inka Road System.* New York: Academic Press.

Hyslop, J. (1990). *Inka Settlement Planning.* Austin: University of Texas Press.

Jadán, M. (2018). Apropiación Inca en la cordillera de Chilla suroeste de los Andes del Ecuador: el caso del sitio Guiñayzhu Site. *Arqueología Iberoamericana* **37**, 13–22.

Julien, C. (1987). Las tumbas de Sacsahuaman y el estilo Cuzco-Inca. *Ñawpa Pacha* **25**(1), 2–125.

Julien, C. (1988). How Inca decimal administration worked. *Ethnohistory* **35** (3), 257–279.

Julien, C. (1998). Coca production on the Inca frontier: the Yungas of Chuquioma. *Andean Past* **5**, 129–160.

LaLone, M., & D. LaLone. (1987). The Inka state in the southern highlands: state administrative and production enclaves. *Ethnohistory* **34**(1), 47–62.

Lechtman, H. (1976). A metallurgical survey in the Peruvian Andes. *Journal of Field Archaeology* **3**, 1–24.

Levillier, R. (1935–1942). *Don Francisco de Toledo, supremo organizador del Perú: Su vida, su obra (1515–1582).* Madrid: Espasa-Calpe.

Mackey, C. (2010). The socioeconomic and ideological transformation of Farfán under Inka rule. In M. Malpass & S. Alconini, eds., *Distant Provinces in the Inka Empire: Towards a Deeper Understanding of Inka Imperialism,* pp. 221–259. Iowa City: University of Iowa Press.

Mackey, C., & A. Nelson. (2020). *Life, Death and Burial Practices During the Inka Occupation of Farfán, on Perú's North Coast.* Andean Past Monograph 6. Orono: Digital Commons, University of Maine.

Mackey, C. & W. D. Sapp (2022). El Algarrobal De Moro: A Lower-level Administrative Center in the Jequetepeque Valley on Peru's North Coast. *Ñawpa Pacha* **42**(1), 33–61.

Makowski, K. (2002). Arquitectura, estilo e identidad en el Horizonte Tardío: el sitio de Pueblo Viejo-Pucará, Valle de Lurín. *Boletín de Arqueología PUCP* **6**, 137–170.

Makowski, K. (2014). Pachacamac – Old Wak'a or Inka Syncretic Deity?: Imperial Transformation of the Sacred Landscape in the Lower Ychsma (Lurín) Valley. In T. Bray, ed., *The Archaeology of Wak'as: Explorations of the Sacred in the Pre-Columbian Andes,* pp. 127–166. Boulder: University Press of Colorado.

Mannheim, B. (1991). *The Language of the Inka since the European Invasion.* Austin: University of Texas Press.

Marcus, J. (2016). *Coastal Ecosystems and Economic Strategies at Cerro Azul, Peru: The Study of a Late Intermediate Kingdom.* Ann Arbor: University of Michigan Museum of Anthropological Archaeology.

Marcus, J., Matos Mendieta, R., & M. Rostworowski de Diez Canseco. (1985). Arquitectura Inca de Cerro Azul, Valle de Cañete. *Revista del Museo Nacional* **47**, 125–138.

Marsh, E., Kidd, R., Ogburn D., & V. Durán. (2017). Dating the expansion of the Inca Empire: Bayesian models from Ecuador and Argentina. *Radiocarbon* **59** (1), 117–140.

Martin, A. (2010). Trade and social complexity in coastal Ecuador from Formative times to European contact. *Journal of Field Archaeology* **35**(1), 40–57.

Marx, K. (1906[1867]). *Capital: A Critique of Political Economy*, Volume 1. Chicago: Charles H. Kerr & Co.

Mayer, E. (2002). *The Articulated Peasant: Household Economies in the Andes*. Boulder: Westview Press.

McEwan, G., Gibaja, A., & M. Chatfield. (2005). Arquitectura monumental en el Cuzco del Periodo Intermedio Tardío: evidencias de continuidades en la reciprocidad ritual y el manejo administrativo entre los horizontes Medio y Tardío. *Boletín de Arqueología PUCP* **9**, 257–280.

Merluzzi, M. (2003). *Politica e governo nel Nuovo Mondo. Francisco de Toledo viceré del Perù (1569–1581)*. Rome: Carocci.

Mignone, P. (2023). Minas, tambos, centros administrativos y montanas en red. Análisis de las interacciones socio-espaciales en el Norte de Argentino durante el *tahuantinsuyu*. *Ñawpa Pacha* **43**(1), 88–119.

Montalvo-Puente, C., Lago, G., Cardarelli, L., & J. Pérez-Molina. (2023). Money or ingots? Metrological research on pre-contact Ecuadorian "axe-monies." *Journal of Archaeological Science: Reports* **49**, 103976.

Morris, C., & D. Thompson. (1985). *Huánuco Pampa: An Inca City and Its Hinterland*. New York: Thames and Hudson.

Morris, C., & J. I. Santillana. (2007). The Inka Transformation of the Chincha Capital. In R. Burger, C. Morris, and R. Matos, eds., *Variations in the Expression of Inka Power*, pp. 135–163. Washington: Dumbarton Oaks.

Morris, C., Covey, R. A., & P. Stein. (2011). *The Huánuco Pampa Archaeological Project. Vol. 1: The Plaza and Palace Complex*. Anthropological Papers of the American Museum of Natural History 96. New York: American Museum of Natural History.

Moseley, M., & K. Day, eds. (1982). *Chan Chan: Andean Desert City*. Santa Fe: School for Advanced Research.

Murra, J. (1956). The Economic Organization of the Inca State. PhD dissertation, University of Chicago.

Murra, J., ed. (1967[1562]). *Visita de la provincia de León de Huánuco en 1562 Iñigo Ortiz de Zúñiga, visitador, tomo I*. Huánuco: Universidad Nacional Hermilio Valdizán.

Murra, J., ed. (1972[1562]). *Visita de la provincia de León de Huánuco en 1562 Iñigo Ortiz de Zúñiga, visitador, tomo II*. Huánuco: Universidad Nacional Hermilio Valdizán.

Murra, J. (1986). The expansion of the Inka state: armies, wars, and rebellions. In J. Murra, N. Wachtel, and J. Revel, eds., *Anthropological History of Andean Polities*, pp. 49–58. New York: Cambridge University Press.

Murra, J. (2017[1969]). *Reciprocity and Redistribution in Andean Civilizations: The 1969 Lewis Henry Morgan Lectures*. Prepared by F. Y. Wolf and H. Lechtman. Chicago: Hau Books.

Netherly, P. (1984). The management of late Andean irrigation systems on the north coast of Peru. *American Antiquity* **49**(2), 227–254.

Nielsen, A. (2021). Rest areas and long-distance caravans: ethnoarchaeological notes from the southern Andes. In P. Clarkson and C. Santoro, eds., *Caravans in Socio-Cultural Perspective*, pp. 20–38. New York: Routledge.

Ogburn, D. (2004). Evidence for long-distance transportation of building stones in the Inka Empire, from Cuzco, Peru to Saraguro, Ecuador. *Latin American Antiquity* **15**(4), 419–439.

Ogburn, D., Connell, S., & C. Gifford. (2009). Provisioning of the Inka army in wartime: obsidian procurement in Pambamarca, Ecuador. *Journal of Archaeological Science* **36**, 740–751.

Ondegardo, P. de. (1940[1561]). Informe del licenciado Juan Polo de Ondegardo al licenciado Briviesca de Muñatones sobre la perpetuidad de las encomiendas en el Perú. *Revista histórica* **13**, 125–196.

Pillsbury, J. (1996). The thorny oyster and the origins of empire: implications of recently uncovered Spondylus imagery from Chan Chan, Peru. *Latin American Antiquity* **7**(4), 313–340.

Pizarro, H. (1968[1533]). Carta de Hernando Pizarro a los magnificos señores oidores de la Audiencia Real … In *Biblioteca peruana: El Perú a través de los siglos, primera serie, tomo 1*, 117–130. Lima: Editores Técnicos Asociados.

Prescott, W. (1847). *History of the Conquest of Peru, with a Preliminary View of the Civilization of the Incas*. London: Richard Bentley.

Prieto, G., & D. Sandweiss, eds. (2020). *Maritime Communities of the Ancient Andes*. Gainesville: University Press of Florida.

Quave, K. (2012). Labor and Domestic Economy on the Royal Estate in the Inka Imperial Heartland (Maras, Cuzco, Peru). PhD dissertation, Southern Methodist University.

Quave, K. (2017). Imperial-style ceramic production on a royal estate in the Inka heartland (Cuzco, Peru). *Latin American Antiquity* **28**(4), 599–608.

Quave, K. (2018). Royal estates and imperial centers in the Cuzco Region. In S. Alconini and R. A. Covey, eds., *The Oxford Handbook of the Incas*, pp. 101–119. New York: Oxford University Press.

Quave, K., & R. A. Covey. (2015). The material remains of Inca power among imperial heartland communities. *Tribus* Special Edition, 111–127.

Quave, K., Covey, R. A., & K. Durand Caceres. (2018). Archaeological investigations at Yunkaray (Cuzco, Peru): reconstructing the rise and fall of an early Inca rival (AD 1050–1450). *Journal of Field Archaeology* **43**(4), 332–343.

Rostworowski, M. (1970). Mercaderes del Valle de Chincha en la época prehispánica: Un documento y unos comentarios. *Revista Española de Antropología Americana* **5**, 135–177.

Rostworowski, M. (1977). *Etnía y Sociedad*. Lima: Instituto de Estudios Peruanos.

Rostworowski, M., ed. (1988). *Conflicts over Coca Fields in Sixteenth-Century Perú*. Ann Arbor: University of Michigan Museum of Anthropology.

Rostworowski, M. (1993). *Ensayos de historia andina*. Lima: Instituto de Estudios Peruanos.

Rostworowski, M. (1999). *Historia del Tahuantinsuyu*. Lima: Insituto de Estudios Peruanos.

Rowe, J. (1948). The Kingdom of Chimor. *Acta Americana* **6**(1–2), 26–59.

Salazar, L., Burger, R., Forst, J., *et al.* (2023). Insights into the genetic histories and lifeways of Machu Picchu's occupants. *Science Advances* **9**(30), eadg3377.

Salomon, F. (2007[1986]). *Native Lords of Quito in the Age of the Incas: the Political Economy of North-Andean Chiefdoms*. Cambridge: Cambridge University Press.

Sámano-Xérez Report. (1968[1527]). Relación. In R. Porras Barrenechea, ed., *Cuadernos de Historia del Perú*. No. 2, pp. 63–68. Paris: Imprimieres Les Preses Modernas.

Sancho de la Hoz, P. (1968[1534]). Relación para su Majestad. In *Biblioteca peruana: El Perú a través de los siglos, primera serie, vol. 1*, 275–343. Lima: Editores Técnicos Asociados.

Sandweiss, D. (1992). The Archaeology of Chincha Fishermen: Specialization and Status in Inka Peru. *Bulletin of the Carnegie Museum of Natural History*, **29**.

Sandweiss, D., & D. Reid. (2016). Negotiated subjugation: maritime trade and the incorporation of Chincha into the Inca Empire. *The Journal of Island and Coastal Archaeology* **11**(3), 311–325.

Santillán, H. de. (1879[1563]). Relación del origen, descendencia, política y gobierno de los Incas. In *Tres Relaciones de Antigüedades Peruanas*, pp. 15–185. Madrid: Ministerio de Fomento.

Santo Tomás, D. (1560). Lexicon, o vocabulario de la lengua general del Perv... Valladolid: Francisco Fernandez de Cordoua.

Schjellerup, I. (2015). Over the mountains, down into the ceja de selva: Inka strategies and impacts in the Chachapoyas region. In I. Shimada, ed., *The Inka Empire: A Multidisciplinary Approach*, pp. 307–323. Austin: University of Texas Press.

Shady, R., Narváez J., & S. López. (2000). La antigüedad del uso del quipu como escritura: las evidencias de la Huaca San Marcos. *Boletín del Museo de Arqueología y Antropología, Universidad Nacional Mayor de San Marcos* **3** (10), 2–23.

Shimada, I. (1996). Sicán metallurgy and its cross-craft relationships. *Boletín del Museo del Oro* **41**, 27–61.

Shimada, I., & J. Merkel. (2021). Naipes: functions and significance of Middle Sicán standardized sheetmetal artifacts. *Ñawpa Pacha* **41**(2), 1–39.

Smith, A. (1776). *An Inquiry into the Nature and Causes of the Wealth of Nations*. London: W. Stratham.

Snead, J. (1992). Imperial infrastructure and the Inka state storage system. In T. Y. LeVine, ed., Inka Storage Systems, pp. 62–106. Norman: University of Oklahoma Press.

Stanish, C. (1989). Household archeology: testing models of zonal complementarity in the south central Andes. *American Anthropologist* **91**(1), 7–24.

Stanish, C. (2003). *Ancient Titicaca: The Evolution of Complex Society in Southern Peru and Northern Bolivia*. Berkeley: University of California Press.

Tello, J. C. (1952). *Presente y future del Museo Nacional*. Lima: Instituto Cultural "Julio C. Tello."

Topic, J. (2003). From stewards to bureaucrats: architecture and information flow at Chan Chan, Peru. *Latin American Antiquity* **14**(3), 243–274.

Topic, J. (2013). Exchange on the equatorial frontier: a comparison of Ecuador and northern Peru. In K. Hirth and J. Pillsbury, eds., *Merchants, Markets, and Exchange in the Pre-Columbian World*, pp. 335–472. Washington: Dumbarton Oaks.

Topic, J., & T. Topic. (1993). A summary of the Inca occupation of Huamachuco. In M. Malpass, ed., *Provincial Inca: Archaeological and Ethnohistorical Assessment of the Impact of the Inca State*, pp. 17–43. Iowa City: University of Iowa Press.

Urton, G., & A. Chu. (2015). Accounting in the King's storehouse: the Inkawasi khipu archive. *Latin American Antiquity* **26**(4), 512–529.

Valdez, L., & K. Bettcher. (2022). The founding of the Inca provincial center of Tambo Viejo, Acarí, Perú. *Ñawpa Pacha* **43**(2), 249–278.

Vega, A. de, Guacra Páucar, F., Lima Illa, C., *et al.* (1965[c. 1580]). La descripción que se hizo en la provincia de Xauxa por la instruction de S. M. ... In M. Jimenez de la Espada, ed., *Relaciones Geográficas de Indias–Perú*, tomo I, pp. 166–172. Madrid: Ediciones Atlas.

Villar Quintana, A. (2021). Instalaciones Incas en la Cuenca del Utcubamba (Amazonas-Perú). *Arkinka* **301**, 72–87.

Vogel, M. (2018). New research on the late prehistoric coastal polities of northern Peru. *Journal of Archaeological Research* **26**(2), 165–195.

Williams, V. (2004). Poder estatal y cultura material en el Kollasuyu. *Boletín de Arqeuología PUCP* **8**, 209–245.

Yaeger, J., & J. M. López-Bejarano. (2018). Inca sacred landscapes in the Titicaca Basin. In S. Alconini and R. A. Covey, eds., *The Oxford Handbook of the Incas*, pp. 541–558. New York: Oxford University Press.

Zori, C. (2011). Metals for the Inka: Craft Production and Empire in the Quebrada de Tarapacá, Northern Chile. Dissertation, University of California, Los Angeles.

Zori, C., Brant E., & M. Uribe Rodríguez. (2017). Empires as social networks: roads, connectedness, and the Inka incorporation of northern Chile. *Ñawpa Pacha* **37**(1), 1–23.

Acknowledgments

We would like to thank the series editors, Tim Earle, Ken Hirth, and Emily J. Kate, for the invitation to develop this Element, and for their constant encouragement throughout the process. Their insights and those of three anonymous reviewers were instrumental in editing the final manuscript. Dalton would like to thank the American Museum of Natural History for support while writing the manuscript and for permission to use images from their archives. Sonia Alconini, Liz Arkush, Sofia Chacaltana, János Gyarmati, Tim Earle, Carlos Montalvo-Puente, Lauren Pratt, and Izumi Shimada generously shared images from their research, which greatly enrich the visual narrative that we are able to offer. Finally, we are grateful for the tireless efforts of colleagues across the Andes, whose fieldwork and analysis informs this study – and hope we have done justice to a large and growing literature.

Cambridge Elements ⹅

Ancient and Pre-modern Economies

Kenneth G. Hirth
The Pennsylvania State University
Ken Hirth's research focuses on the development of ranked and state-level societies in the New World. He is interested in political economy and how forms of resource control lead to the development of structural inequalities. Topics of special interest include: exchange systems, craft production, settlement patterns, and preindustrial urbanism. Methodological interests include: lithic technology and use-wear, ceramics, and spatial analysis.

Timothy Earle
Northwestern University
Timothy Earle is an economic anthropologist specializing in the archaeological studies of social inequality, leadership, and political economy in early chiefdoms and states. He has conducted field projects in Polynesia, Peru, Argentina, Denmark, and Hungary. Having studied the emergence of social complexity in three world regions, his work is comparative, searching for the causes of alternative pathways to centralized power.

Emily J. Kate
University of Vienna
Emily Kate is bioarchaeologist with training in radiocarbon dating, isotopic studies, human osteology, and paleodemography. Having worked with projects from Latin America and Europe, her interests include the manner in which paleodietary trends can be used to assess shifts in social and political structure, the affect of migration on societies, and the refinement of regional chronologies through radiocarbon programs.

About the Series
Elements in Ancient and Pre-modern Economies is committed to critical scholarship on the comparative economies of traditional societies. Volumes either focus on case studies of well documented societies, providing information on domestic and institutional economies, or provide comparative analyses of topical issues related to economic function. Each Element adopts an innovative and interdisciplinary view of culture and economy, offering authoritative discussions of how societies survived and thrived throughout human history.

Cambridge Elements ⁼

Ancient and Pre-modern Economies

Elements in the Series

Ancient and Pre-modern Economies of the North American Pacific Northwest
Anna Marie Prentiss

The Aztec Economy
Frances F. Berdan

Shell Money: A Comparative Study
Mikael Fauvelle

A Historical Ethnography of the Enga Economy of Papua New Guinea
Polly Wiessner, Akii Tumu and Nitze Pupu

Ancient Maya Economies
Scott R. Hutson

Nordic Bronze Age Economies
Christian Horn, Knut Ivar Austvoll, Magnus Artursson and Johan Ling

Economies of the Inca World
R. Alan Covey and Jordan Dalton

A full series listing is available at: www.cambridge.org/EAPE

Printed in the United States
by Baker & Taylor Publisher Services